Spirit Dance at Meziadin

Spirit Dance at Meziadin:

Joseph Gosnell and the Nisga'a Treaty

Alex Rose

Principal photography by
Gary Fiegehen

HARBOUR PUBLISHING

Harbour Publishing, P.O. Box 219, Madeira Park, BC, V0N 2H0

We acknowledge the financial support of the Government of Canada through the Book Publishing Industry Development Program for our publishing activities. We further acknowledge the support of the Canada Council for the Arts and the Province of British Columbia through the British Columbia Arts Council for our publishing program.

THE CANADA COUNCIL | LE CONSEIL DES ARTS
FOR THE ARTS | DU CANADA
SINCE 1957 | DEPUIS 1957

Printed in Canada
Edited by Betty Keller and Irene Niechoda
Cover photos by Gary Fiegehen
Page design and layout by Martin Nichols
In photo credits, *RBCM* = Royal British Columbia Museum in Victoria

Canadian Cataloguing in Publication Data

Rose, Alex.
    Spirit dance at Meziadin

    ISBN 1-55017-244-1

    1. Gosnell, Joe. 2. Canada. Nisga'a final agreement. 3. Nis_ga'a Indians—Biography.* I. Title.
E99.N734G67 2000   343.71'025'0899741   C00-910771-1

For Joanne, Caroline and Alexandra

Table of Contents

Acknowledgements

My father, Ron Rose, who encouraged and advised throughout. My editor, Betty Keller, who made crucial contributions to the final shape of this book. I relied on three books in particular for historical background: Robin Fisher's *Contact and Conflict*, Paul Tennant's *Aboriginal Peoples and Politics* and Daniel Raunet's *Without Surrender, Without Consent*. And the following, all of whom endured my work habits with an implacable patience: Esther Adams, Jim Adams, Jim Aldridge, Collier Azak, Lee Bacchus, Peter Baird, Thomas Berger, Carole Blackburn, Frank Calder, David Carruthers, Ken Coates, Gary Fiegehen, Robin Fisher, Ian Gill, Terry Glavin, Joseph Gosnell, Eric Grandison, Mike Guy, Hamar Foster, Daniel Francis, Peter Hill, Mark Hume, Stephen Hume, Adele Hurley, Sandy Kovacs, Jennifer Lang, Rod Link, Kirsti Medig, Rod Mickleburgh, Jeff Nagel, Patrick Nagle, Peter Pearse, Tony Pearse, Chris Rose, Jim Skipp, Dr. Isaac Sobol, Bob Spence, Graham Smith, Alver Tait, Doug Wanamaker, Gloria Williams and Milton K. Wong.

Preface

In 1989 I was hired by the Nisga'a Tribal Council to help explain the 130-year-old Nisga'a quest to settle the "Land Question" to the Canadian people. The Nisga'a of northwestern British Columbia were pressing to settle their land claim and sign a treaty as compensation for lands appropriated by a settler society a century earlier. After a fierce and prolonged debate that divided the country, Chief Joseph Gosnell saw the Nisga'a treaty ratified on Parliament Hill in the spring of 2000.

As I was to learn first-hand, treaty making and aboriginal rights remain complicated and vexatious issues that lie at the heart of Canadian history. In these pages, I make no attempt to play historian, anthropologist or constitutional lawyer. What follows, with the exception of some background explanation, are simply the events as I witnessed them, a sharing of my memories of the Nisga'a people during a tumultuous period of history.

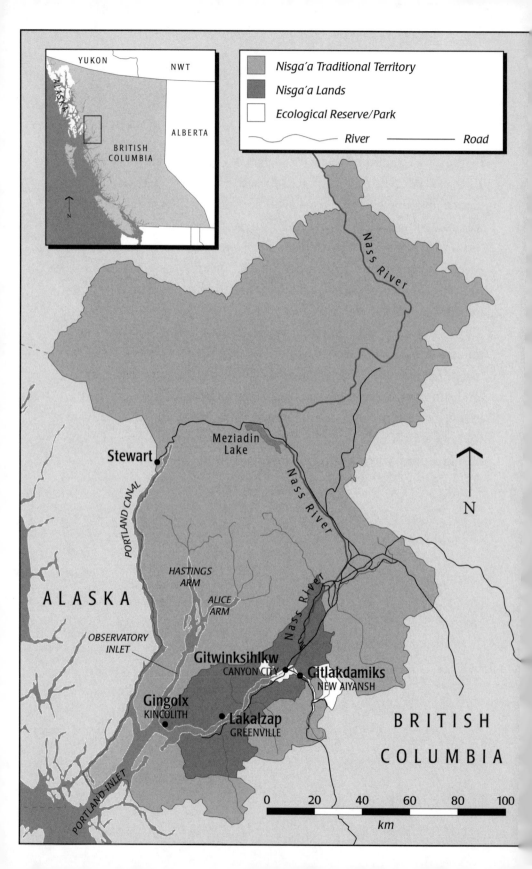

CHAPTER ONE:

The Treaty

I n January 1887 a delegation of chiefs from the Nisga'a and Tsimshian peoples of northern British Columbia, seeking restitution from a government that had stolen their lands without a treaty or compensation, arrived by steamship in Victoria's inner harbour. They were met by Premier William Smithe who received them with a blunt rebuke. "When the white man first came among you," he told them, "you were little better than wild beasts of the field."

The official records in the government archives show that Smithe did agree to meet them in his home and, in response to a demand by Nisga'a chiefs Arthur Gurney, John Wesley and Charles Barton, promised an inquiry into the Indians' "views, wishes and complaints" if any. But it is obvious from the tone of Smithe's instructions to his commissioners that

Detail of a Norman Tait totem pole.
Gary Fiegehen photo

he had no intention of seriously consider-ing the vexing questions of land title or treaty making. And this was the attitude that paralyzed Nisga'a aspirations for more than one hundred years.

Shocking today, Smithe's repudiation, rooted in colonial notions of race, accu-rately reflected the dominant ideology of the British colonizers who had an urgent sense of a mission to civilize the Nisga'a and other "heathens" of British Columbia. Born in England, Smithe came to BC in 1862 and settled on a farm near Cowichan Lake on Vancouver Island. As the province's seventh premier Smithe passed anti-Asian legislation and limited the size of Indian reserves in favour of white settlers. Many of the reserves had been surveyed and created by Lands and Works Commissioner Joseph Trutch, a fellow Englishman who shared the racist assumptions of the day. To Trutch, aboriginal people were a nui-sance, an impediment to progress, and their control of key pieces of land a seri-ous economic disadvantage to settler soci-ety. Not the least interested in settling the Indian land question, he denied that abo-riginal people had any rights to the land at all, explaining in 1872, "Our problem here in British Columbia is nothing other than 30,000 savages."

Top: Premier William Smithe, ca 1885.
BC Archives H-00791
Bottom: Lands and Works Commissioner
Joseph Trutch, 1875. *BC Archives F-07196*

One hundred and eleven years after that delegation was turned back by Premier Smithe, on December 2, 1998, the Nisga'a were back on the front lawn of the Parliament Buildings, this time to a very different reception. Invited to launch debate on Bill 51: The Nisga'a Final Agreement Act, Chief Joseph Gosnell and a delegation of Nisga'a people were gathered on the front steps of the legislature, to be greeted and welcomed inside by NDP Premier Glen Clark. In a dramatic turn of history, the charismatic Gosnell and a procession of one hundred Nisga'a moved slowly through the ceremonial gates and into the ornate legislative rotunda, where they gathered to call out the names of their leaders who had died during the century-old struggle for justice.

Minutes later, the doors of the legislative chamber were thrown back and Chief Gosnell, flanked by fellow Nisga'a,

On December 2, 1998, the doors of the BC Legislature were ceremonially thrown open to welcome Joseph Gosnell and a contingent of Nisga'a people. *Gary Fiegehen photo*

Edmond Wright and Nelson Leeson, took his place at the gold bar of the House. An overflow crowd in the public gallery leaned forward as Gosnell—his red-and-black button blanket draped over his dark business suit—looked across at the elected representatives and began to speak in long, rolling sentences, punctuating them with a series of syncopated refrains. As he spoke, the chamber seemed a little larger than before, political opponents of the treaty that much smaller.

> Madame Speaker, Honourable Members, ladies and gentlemen. Today marks a turning point in the history of British Columbia. Today, aboriginal and non-aboriginal people are coming together to decide the future of this province. I am talking about the Nisga'a Treaty—a triumph for all British Columbians and a beacon of hope for aboriginal people around the world. A triumph, I believe, which proves to the world that reasonable people can sit down and settle historical wrongs. It proves that a modern society can correct the mistakes of the past. As British Columbians, as Canadians, we should all be very proud. A triumph because, under the treaty the Nisga'a people will join Canada and British Columbia as free citizens—full and equal participants in the social, economic and political life of this province, of this country. A triumph because under the treaty we will no longer be wards of the state, no longer beggars in our own lands.
>
> A triumph because under the treaty we will collectively own about 2,000 square kilometres of land, far exceeding the postage-stamp reserves set aside for us by colonial governments. We will once again govern ourselves by our own institutions but within the context of Canadian law.
>
> It is a triumph because under the treaty we will be

allowed to make our own mistakes, to savour our own victories, to stand on our own feet once again. A triumph because, clause by clause, the Nisga'a Treaty emphasizes self-reliance, personal responsibility and modern education. It also encourages, for the first time, investment in Nisga'a lands and resources and allows us to pursue meaningful employment from the resources of our own territory for our own people. To investors it provides economic certainty and gives us a fighting chance to establish legitimate economic independence—to prosper in common with our non-aboriginal neighbours in a new and proud Canada.

A triumph, Madame Speaker and Honourable Members, because the treaty proves beyond all doubt that negotiations—not lawsuits, not blockades, not violence—are the most effective, most honourable way to

Nisga'a leaders Edmond Wright (left) and Nelson Leeson (right) flank Joseph Gosnell as he delivers an emotional speech to the BC Legislature on December 2, 1998. *Diana Nethercott photo*

resolve aboriginal issues in this country. A triumph that
signals the end of the *Indian Act*—the end of more than
a century of humiliation, degradation and despair.

In 1887, my ancestors made an epic journey from the
Nass River here to Victoria's inner harbour. Determined
to settle the Land Question, they were met by a premier
who barred them from the legislature. He was blunt.
Premier Smithe rejected all our aspirations to settle the
Land Question. Then he made this pronouncement, and
I quote: "When the white man first came among you, you
were little better than wild beasts of the field." Wild
beasts of the field! Little wonder then, that this brutal
racism was soon translated into narrow policies which
plunged British Columbia into a century of darkness for
the Nisga'a and other aboriginal people.

Like many colonists of the day, Premier Smithe did not
know, or care to know, that the Nisga'a is an old nation,
as old as any in Europe. From time immemorial, our oral
literature, passed down from generation to generation,
records the story of the way the Nisga'a people were
placed on earth, entrusted with the care and protection
of our land. Through the ages, we lived a settled life in villages along the Nass River. We lived in large, cedar-
planked houses, fronted with totem poles depicting the
great heraldry and the family crests of our nobility. We
thrived from the bounty of the sea, the river, the forest
and the mountains.

We governed ourselves according to *Ayuukhl Nisga'a*,
the code of our own strict and ancient laws of property
ownership, succession and civil order. Our first encounters with Europeans were friendly. We welcomed these
strange visitors, visitors who never left. The Europeans

also valued their encounters with us. They thought we were fair and tough entrepreneurs and, no doubt today, negotiators. In 1832, traders from the Hudson's Bay Company found us living, in their words, in "two storey wooden houses the equal of any in Europe." For a time, we continued to prosper.

But there were dark days to come. Between the late 1700s and the mid-1800s, the Nisga'a people, like so many other coastal nations of the time, were devastated by European diseases such as smallpox, measles and fevers. Our population, once 30,000, dwindled to about 800 people. Today, I am pleased to report, our population is growing again. Today, we number 5,500 people.

We took to heart the promises of King George III, set out in the Royal Proclamation of 1763, that our lands would not be taken without our permission, and that treaty making was the way the Nisga'a would become part of this new nation. We continued to follow our *ayuukhl*, our code of laws. We vowed to obey the white man's laws, too, and we expected him to obey his own law—and to respect ours.

But the Europeans would not obey their own laws, and continued to trespass on our lands. The King's governments continued to take our lands from us, until we were told that all of our lands had come to belong to the Crown, and even the tiny bits of land that enclosed our villages were not ours, but belonged to the government. Still, we kept faith that the rule of law would prevail one day, that justice would be done. That one day, the Land Question would be settled fairly and honourably.

In 1913, the Nisga'a Land Committee drafted a petition to London. The petition contained a declaration of our traditional land ownership and governance and it contained the critical affirmation that, in the new British colony, our land ownership would be respected. In part the petition said:

"We are not opposed to the coming of the white people into our territory, provided this be carried out justly and in accordance with the British principles embodied in the Royal Proclamation. If therefore as we expect the aboriginal rights which we claim should be established by the decision of His Majesty's Privy Council, we would be prepared to take a moderate and reasonable position. In that event, while claiming the right to decide for ourselves, the terms upon which we would deal with our territory, we would be willing that all matters outstanding between the province and ourselves should be finally adjusted by some equitable method to be agreed upon which should include representation of the Indian Tribes upon any Commission which might then be appointed."

The above statement was unanimously adopted at a meeting of the Nisga'a Nation or Tribe of Indians held at the village of Gingolx on the twenty-second day of January, 1913. Sadly, this was not to be the case.

Also in 1913, Duncan Campbell Scott became deputy superintendent of Indian Affairs. His narrow vision of assimilation dominated federal aboriginal policy for years and years to come and was later codified as the *Indian Act*. Mr. Scott said, "I want to get rid of the Indian problem. Our objective is to continue until there is not a single Indian in Canada that has not been absorbed into the body politic and there is no Indian question." One of this man's earliest efforts was to undermine the influence of the Nisga'a petition to London and to deflect attention away from political action. But these men, Smithe and Scott, failed and are now deservedly only dusty footnotes in history. Still, the situation of the Nisga'a worsened. In 1927 Canada passed a law to prevent us from pursuing our land claims, from hiring lawyers to plead our case. At the same time, our central institution of tribal government, the potlatch system (*yuukw*), was outlawed by an Act of Parliament. It was against the law for us to give presents to one another during our ceremonies, which our laws instructed us to do. It was even made illegal for us to sing, to dance.

But still we never gave up. And then finally, under the leadership of President Emeritus Frank Calder, the Nisga'a Land Committee was reborn as the Nisga'a Tribal Council in 1955. In 1968, we took our Land Question to the BC Supreme Court. We lost but appealed to the Supreme Court of Canada, where in 1973—in what is now known as the Calder Case—the judges ruled that aboriginal title existed prior to Confederation. This initiated the modern-day process of land claims negotiations. The government of Canada agreed it was best to negotiate modern-day treaties. Canada agreed it was time to build a new relationship, based on trust, respect and the rule of law. In time, as you well know, Madame Speaker, the province of British Columbia came to the negotiating table as well. For the past twenty-five years, in good faith, the Nisga'a struggled to negotiate this treaty and finally, it was initialled in August in our village of Gitlakdamiks.

How the world has changed. Two days ago and one hundred and eleven years after Smithe's rejection, I walked up the steps of this legislature as the sound of

Nisga'a drumming and singing filled the rotunda. To the Nisga'a people, it was a joyous sound, the sound of freedom. What does *freedom* mean? I looked it up in the dictionary. It means "the state or condition of being free, the condition of not being under another's control; the power to do, say, or think as one pleases."

Our people have enjoyed the hospitality and warmth of this legislature, this capital city, its sights and its people—in churches, schools, malls, streets and public places. Our people have been embraced, welcomed and congratulated by the people of British Columbia, Madame Speaker. People sometimes wonder why we have struggled so long to sign a treaty. Why, we are asked, did our elders and elected officials dedicate their lives to a resolution of the Land Question? What is it about a treaty? To us, a treaty is a sacred instrument. It represents an understanding between distinct cultures and shows respect for each other's way of life. We know we are here for a long time together. A treaty stands as a symbol of high idealism in a divided world. That is why we have fought so long, and so hard. I have been asked, has it been worth it? Yes, a resounding yes. But, believe me, it has been a long and hard-fought battle. Some may have heard us say that a generation of Nisga'a men and women has grown old at the negotiating table. Sadly, it is very, very true.

Let me share some personal history. When I began this process I was a young man. When I first became involved in our Tribal Council, I was twenty-five years old. Now I am sixty-three. Today, my hair is grey. The terms of six prime ministers chart the years I have grown old at the negotiating table:

The Right Honourable Pierre Trudeau,
Joe Clark,
John Turner,
Brian Mulroney,
Kim Campbell and
Jean Chrétien.
And five British Columbia premiers:
Bill Bennett,
William Vander Zalm,
Rita Johnson,
Mike Harcourt and
Glen Clark.

I will spare you the list of deputy ministers, senior bureaucrats and other officials we have met across the table during the past quarter century. Their names would paper the walls of this chamber. At least twice, I'd bet.

We are not naive. We know that some people do not want this treaty. We know there are naysayers, some sitting here today. We know there are some who say Canada and BC are "giving" us too much. And a few who want to re-open negotiations in order to "give" us less. Others—still upholding the values of Smithe and Scott—are practising a willful ignorance. This colonial attitude is fanning the flames of fear and ignorance in this province and reigniting a poisonous attitude so familiar to aboriginal people.

But these are desperate tactics doomed to fail. By playing politics with the aspirations of aboriginal people these naysayers are blighting the promise of the Nisga'a Treaty—not only for us, but for non-aboriginal people as well. Because, Madame Speaker, this is about people. We are not numbers. In this legislative debate, you will be dealing with the lives of our people, with the futures of our individual people. This is about the legitimate aspirations of people no longer willing to step aside or be marginalized. We intend to be free and equal citizens, Madame Speaker. Witness the flags that have been waved in this chamber over the past two days by the Nisga'a people of British Columbia, the Nisga'a people of Canada.

Now, on the eve of the fiftieth anniversary of the Declaration of Human Rights, this legislature embarks on a great debate about aboriginal rights. The Nisga'a people welcome that debate—one of the most important in the modern history of British Columbia. And we have every confidence that elected members of this legislature will look beyond narrow politics to correct a shameful and historic wrong. I ask every Honourable Member to search their hearts deeply and to allow the light of our message to guide their decision.

We have worked for justice for more than a century. Now, it is time to ratify the Nisga'a Treaty, for aboriginal and non-aboriginal people to come together and write a new chapter in the history of our Nation, our province, our country and, indeed, the world. The world is our witness. Be strong. Be steadfast. Be true.

As Gosnell finished speaking, the legislature and public gallery turned silent for a moment before people stood to break into waves of extended applause. On all sides of the House, MLAs stood in tears as the sound of Nisga'a drumming reverberated throughout the rotunda. But by next morning this shining moment had been allocated to memory as the House began debate on the bill (C-32) to ratify the Nisga'a Treaty. Fierce and ideologically driven, this debate would drag on for almost five months until, on April 22, 1999, Premier Clark, rewriting the rules to cut off debate, invoked closure so the treaty could be passed along party lines. Howls of protest, first heard from BC Liberal Opposition Leader Gordon Campbell, would follow the treaty across Canada to the scene of the federal debate on Parliament Hill. Much of this firestorm was due to the widely held perception that the treaty was a "done deal" before the debate even began in the provincial legislature. In Ottawa the treaty was backed by the Liberals, who held majorities in both House and Senate, and by the Bloc Québécois (BQ), the New Democratic Party (NDP) and the Progressive Conservatives (PC). However, it was bitterly opposed by the Reform Party—the official opposition— which delayed the treaty's passage for more than forty hours by proposing more than four hundred amendments. After a contentious debate, the House of Commons passed the treaty on December 13, 1999, by a vote of 217 to 48. It was then referred to the Senate.

On April 13, 2000, inside the Senate, Joseph Gosnell sighed with relief as Governor General Adrienne Clarkson gave the treaty royal assent. Fighting back tears, the tired but jubilant Nisga'a chief hurried across the foyer and out into the bright sunlight on the steps of the Senate, where he proclaimed the treaty a triumph for the Nisga'a people and a beacon of hope for aboriginal people around the world. Minutes later, 5,000 miles away in a remote corner of northwestern British Columbia, the Nisga'a people heard the news through a series of excited telephone calls. Reaction was immediate. Waving the Canadian flag, people rushed out into the streets

of their villages to cheer a treaty which had cut the chains of the *Indian Act*.

Although the legal document that spells out this historic treaty is complicated and intimidating to read, the treaty's fundamentals are nevertheless reasonably clear. Under its terms, the Nisga'a will continue to be aboriginal people as defined by the *Constitution Act* of 1982, but since the Canadian Charter of Rights and Freedoms applies to the Nisga'a government and its institutions, they will now also have the rights and protections enjoyed by other Canadian citizens.

The Nisga'a will receive a cash settlement of $487.1 million to be held in a communal trust. From this sum, $51.3 million must be repaid to the federal government over a period of fifteen years to cover monies advanced to the Nisga'a to pay for its twenty-three years of negotiations. Under a complicated fiscal formula, transfer payments to the Nisga'a from Ottawa and Victoria will continue for housing, health care, education and other social programs.

Collectively the Nisga'a now own 1,992 square kilometres of land in the lower Nass Valley, held in fee simple, as well as all the subsurface resources on them. These lands, designated as the Nisga'a core lands or "Nisga'a Lands," include approximately 1,930 square kilometres of transferred Crown

Old meets new. Dressed in traditional regalia, Alvin Aazak uses a cell phone in the Nass River Valley. Moments after the treaty was ratified in Ottawa, cell phones were used to spread the good news to the Nisga'a back home. *Gary Fiegehen photo*

The upper Nass River near its headwaters in
northwestern BC. *Gary Fiegehen photo*

land and 62 square kilometres of former *Indian Act* reserves. Land contained within eighteen Indian reserves outside the core lands, and a small amount of adjacent land, have become Category A fee simple lands; these lands as well as their subsurface resources remain the property of the Nisga'a people. They also own an additional fifteen parcels of fee simple Category B lands, totalling approximately 2.5 square kilometres, but subsurface resources on these lands are still owned by the province and remain under provincial jurisdiction. The "Nisga'a Lands" do not include previously existing fee simple lands or lands subject to agricultural leases and woodlot licences. Individual parcels within the Nisga'a Lands will initially be registered under a Nisga'a land title system but, following a transition period, may be registered under the provincial land title system.

The Nisga'a will be governed by the Nisga'a Lisims Government (central government) and four village governments under a constitution that sets out the terms of governance and recognizes the rights and freedoms of its citizens. The first elections were held in November 2000. Non-Nisga'a citizens living within these lands are not eligible to vote or run for office in elections, but the Nisga'a government is required to consult with them on decisions that significantly and directly affect them. They will be given opportunities to make representations, to vote for or seek election to Nisga'a non-governmental public institutions, and to have the same means of appeal as Nisga'a citizens.

Nisga'a Lands will continue to be part of the Electoral Area "A" in the regional district of Kitimat-Stikine. The Nisga'a and the regional district may enter into servicing agreements or otherwise coordinate their activities with respect to common areas of responsibility.

The Nisga'a government will have the power to make laws required to carry out its responsibilities and exercise its authority. In addition, it may make laws governing such things as Nisga'a citizenship; Nisga'a language and culture; Nisga'a property within the Nisga'a Lands; public order, peace and safety; employment; traffic and transportation; the solemnization of marriages; child and family, social and health services; child custody, adoption and education. In the majority of cases Nisga'a laws will only pertain to Nisga'a citizens, although some local laws, such as traffic and transportation, will apply to other residents. However, federal and provincial laws will continue to apply to Nisga'a citizens and to the Nisga'a Lands, and the relationship between these laws and Nisga'a laws has been clearly set out in the final agreement.

Self-government in action. One of the first sessions at Wilpsi'ayuukhl Nisga'a (legislative building) held in Gitlakdamiks. *Gary Fiegehen photo*

The treaty allows the Nisga'a government to provide policing, correctional and court services within their lands with the approval of the Lieutenant-Governor in Council. A Nisga'a police service will have the full range of police responsibilities and the authority to enforce Nisga'a, provincial and federal laws, including the Criminal Code of Canada, within their lands. Such a force, though independent and accountable, will be required to meet provincial qualifications, training and professional standards. To provide community correctional services, the Nisga'a may enter into agreements with either Canada or British Columbia. Should a Nisga'a court be established, it will adjudicate prosecutions and civil disputes arising under Nisga'a laws and review the administrative decisions of Nisga'a public institutions. Judges will be appointed by the Nisga'a government, according to a method of selection approved by the Lieutenant-Governor in Council, and they will comply with generally recognized principles of judicial fairness, independence and impartiality. In legal proceedings where the accused could face imprisonment under Nisga'a law, he or she may elect to be tried in the Provincial Court of British Columbia. Final decisions by the

Mansell Griffin plays show-and-tell with his drum at the elementary school. Students are bilingual in the Nass Valley, receiving instruction in both Nisga'a and English. *Gary Fiegehen photo*

Nisga'a court may be appealed to the Supreme Court of British Columbia on the same basis as decisions made by British Columbia's provincial court.

The *Indian Act* tax exemption will be eliminated for Nisga'a citizens after a transitional period of eight years for transaction (e.g. sales) taxes and twelve years for other (e.g. income) taxes. Pursuant to a final taxation agreement, the Nisga'a government and Nisga'a village governments will be treated in the same way as municipalities for tax purposes. In addition, the Nisga'a government will have the power to directly tax its citizens within its lands. However, the governments of the Nisga'a, Canada and British Columbia may negotiate tax delegation agreements, and the parties may make agreements to coordinate their respective tax systems.

There will be reasonable public access on Nisga'a public lands for non-commercial purposes such as hunting, fishing and recreation. Provision has also been made for the federal and provincial governments to have access for the delivery or management of government services and emergency response. Likewise, representatives of Nisga'a Lisims Government may, in accordance with the laws of general application, have temporary access to lands other than Nisga'a Lands for similar purposes. However, the Nisga'a Lisims Government may make laws regulating public access for the purposes of public safety, protection of environmental, cultural or historic features, and protection of habitat. They also have the power to make laws relating to environmental assessment and protection, but the environmental standards which they set must meet or exceed federal and provincial standards.

Important cultural sites will be protected through heritage site designations and key geographic features will be renamed

T'aam Anlibaykw (Amoth Lake), a site sacred to
the Nisga'a. *Gary Fiegehen photo*

with Nisga'a names. Victoria's authority and responsibilities over the Nisga'a Memorial Lava Bed Provincial Park and Gingietl Creek Ecological Reserve will continue even though Nisga'a history and culture are, and will be promoted as, the primary cultural features of the Park. Nisga'a citizens have the right to use the lands and resources within the park and eco-logical reserve for traditional purposes.

The province of British Columbia still owns the Nisga'a Highway—the main road through the core lands—and will maintain secondary provincial roads. The province may also acquire portions of Nisga'a Lands to create additional rights-of-way for road or public utility purposes. However, the Nisga'a Lisims Government will regulate and maintain all other roads within the core lands. Existing water licences remain in place. Victoria will establish a Nisga'a water reser-vation of 300,000 cubic decametres of water per year to meet domestic, industrial and agricultural purposes.

The Nisga'a people now own all forest resources on the core lands with an annual allowable cut of 150,000 cubic metres. However, terms of existing licences will remain in effect for a five-year transition period to allow licensees to adjust their operations. Following the transition period, new licences will be issued, and the Nisga'a will manage the forestry and implement forest management standards, pro-vided they meet or exceed provincial standards such as the Forest Practices Code. Provincial laws pertaining to the manufacture of timber products harvested on Crown lands will apply equally to timber harvested on Nisga'a Lands. The treaty also requires the Nisga'a not to build a sawmill for ten years.

The treaty provides for the Nisga'a to receive an annual allocation of approximately 26 percent of the Nass River

salmon run, and in order to participate in this commercial fishing industry, they will receive $11.5 million from Canada and BC. They will sell their salmon subject to the monitoring, enforcement and laws of general application. They also undertake not to build canneries or fish processing plants for eight years.

More specific decisions pertaining to fish and seafood harvests are contained in a Harvest Agreement, separate from the treaty. In the matter of sockeye and pink salmon harvests, this document states that if in any year there are no directed Canadian commercial or recreational fisheries for a species of Nass salmon, it is agreed that a Nisga'a commercial fishery will not be permitted for that species. However, the Nisga'a have the right to harvest steelhead, non-salmon species in the Nass area—halibut, shellfish, crab—and aquatic plants for domestic purposes and subject to conservation requirements.

Nisga'a loggers in the lower Nass Valley. When forest companies first came to the Nass, they had little incentive to employ Nisga'a workers. Now, under the ratified treaty, many Nisga'a will work in the forests. *Gary Fiegehen photo*

Although Ottawa and Victoria retain responsibility for conservation and management of the fisheries and fish habitat according to their respective jurisdictions, the Nisga'a government may make laws to manage the Nisga'a harvest, once fishing plans are approved by the minister of Fisheries and Oceans. The Nisga'a may also conduct enhancement activities for Nass salmon; the Lisims Fisheries Conservation Trust has been set up to promote and conserve Nass fish stocks. To this last initiative Canada will contribute $10 million, with the Nisga'a contributing an additional $3 million.

Within the Nass Wildlife Area the Nisga'a have the right to harvest wildlife for domestic purposes, with specific allocations for moose, grizzly bear and mountain goat. They may also harvest migratory birds. However, since the BC Ministry of Environment, Lands and Parks remains responsible for all

Fisheries technicians at salmon hatchery in Gingolx. The Nisga'a are proud of the award-winning conservation program they designed specifically to protect salmon and other fish stocks. *Gary Fiegehen photo*

wildlife, the Nisga'a must develop an annual management plan subject to ministerial approval and with due regard to conservation requirements and legislation enacted for the purposes of public health and safety. In addition, their right to hunt cannot interfere with other authorized uses of Crown land and does not preclude the Crown from authorizing uses of or disposing of Crown land, subject to certain considerations. The Nisga'a people now have a commercial recreation tenure for guiding, which will also operate under provincial laws. Trapping, too, will continue to be regulated in accordance with provincial laws. Nisga'a citizens who hunt outside the management area will still be subject to provincial laws.

This, in very brief outline, is the treaty that has caused so much controversy, which has become on the one hand an international symbol of the way Canada treats its aboriginal people, while on the other a lightning rod for furious protest. It has forced Canadians to examine a series of uncomfortable truths about their colonial history and challenged decades of accreted learning about this issue. And it represents the biggest shift in the relationship between First Nations and non-aboriginal people in British Columbia since Captain George Vancouver arrived here in 1792 to put this coastline onto the charts.

But while the Nisga'a celebrated the passage of the treaty into law, many Canadians were still asking what right the federal and provincial governments had to "give away" this piece of prime real estate to these aboriginal peoples. Others worried that the treaty violated Canada's constitution, that the treaty had created a special class within our society, that Canadians would no longer be equal before the law. And they asked just who were these Nisga'a people that they should receive these extra privileges.

CHAPTER TWO:

The History

M uch modern treaty making is predicated on a
set of slippery definitions that are still being
defined by the courts. In the case of treaties
between Canada's federal government and
aboriginal peoples, the most fundamental of these terms are
"aboriginal title" and "aboriginal rights"; in essence, both
refer to title, occupation and use of land and resources as
they existed prior to the arrival of European colonial powers.
For the Nisga'a people, proof of aboriginal title meant establishing the exact extent of the land to which they claimed title
and the duration of their occupancy and use of its resources
before Europeans laid claim to it, a difficult task with only
oral history and legend as their authority.

Galsgiyst, in Observatory Inlet, looking south.
Gary Fiegehen photo

The lands to which they laid claim lie in the remote north-western portion of the province, beginning just south of the panhandle of Alaska where, in the shadow of Mount Khutzeymateen, a fjord knifes northeastward into a long line of jagged mountains—the Coast Range. This fjord begins as Portland Inlet, then forms two branches as it swings into a more northerly direction. The most westerly branch is Portland Canal, which forms British Columbia's boundary with the panhandle; the easterly branch is Observatory Inlet. In the wind-whipped waters of Observatory Inlet nature can be a capricious and malignant force, but because these salt-water passages contain rich intertidal habitats and safe harbours they were, for the ancient Nisga'a, a primary workplace where they fished, fought wars, traded goods, met wives and husbands. Every current, bay, souse hole and back eddy was given a special name.

Where Observatory Inlet joins Portland Inlet, the glacier-fed Nass River pours into the sea from the east. The third-largest salmon producing river on the BC Coast, the 380-kilometre-long Nass—the Nisga'a call it Lisims—drains a watershed of 21,567 square kilometres, an area more than three and a half times the size of Prince Edward Island. When treaty talks began, this whole watershed was claimed by the Nisga'a people. It is their traditional hunting and fishing territory, although their settlements are confined to the lower reaches of the river.

Of the four Nisga'a settlements along the Nass, Gingolx (Kincolith) is the smallest and most isolated by its geography. A village of four hundred people, it sits at the mouth of the river on the westernmost tip of the Nisga'a's traditional lands and has no road to connect it to the upriver communities. It is therefore accessible only by float plane, boat, or the twice-

weekly ferry trip to Prince Rupert, five hours away. This is the
northern edge of the Pacific rain forest. Weather systems carried by the Japanese current dump about 250 cm (100 inches) of rain here annually, but the climate is relatively mild,
with winter temperatures hovering near the freezing mark
and summer temperatures in the high teens and low 20s
Celsius. At low to middle elevations in this lower end of the
Nass Valley, the forest cover is comprised of Sitka spruce,
western hemlock and red cedar. However, much of this blanket of giant softwoods—where the largest trees once grew to
heights of over 65 metres and three metres wide at the
base—has been logged over. As the river winds its way along
the valley floor, the boundary between the water and these
ancient conifer forests is marked by stands of cottonwood,
and they also cover many of the larger islands in the river.

Upriver from Gingolx the stream widens into Fishery Bay,
where eulachon, a small type of smelt, return to spawn each

The small Nisga'a village of Gingolx. The landscape
of this isolated coastal community is dominated by
the tall spire of the Anglican church.
Gary Fiegehen photo

year. To the early Nisga'a, the oil extracted from the eulachon provided a rich dietary supplement with reputed curative powers, but it was also a condiment to liven up a steady winter diet of dried salmon, dried berry cakes and dried deer meat. In addition, it was the main item of trade with other aboriginal peoples along elaborate networks of "grease trails" that extended from the coast far into the interior. The grease is rated according to individual taste and preference, the way different kinds of wine are valued in European culture.

Upstream from Fishery Bay and beyond the tiny village (population approximately 1,000) of Lakalzap (Greenville) the river narrows to skirt the vast lava beds that cover the heart of the central Nass River Valley. These beds form a barren plain of jumbled and broken volcanic rock, the kind of landscape that might belong on some distant planet, except

March is eulachon season at Fishery Bay. The rich oil made from the smelt-like fish is considered a delicacy by the Nisga'a. *Gary Fiegehen photo* that there is a slippery mud road running through the middle of it and a line of telephone poles stretches off into the distance and disappears into the horizon. In summer, thin light, short nights and glittering white waterfalls make this an exotic place—the Nisga'a call it *Anhluut'ukwsim Laxmihl Angwinga'asanskwhl Nisga'a*. It was here more than three hundred years ago that the volcano Wilksi Baxhl Mihl erupted and a river of molten rock entombed 2,000 people in a village named Lax Ksi Luux and forced the river to adopt a new course below the mountain wall on the valley's north flank. This volcanic eruption is part of European history as well. In

Memorial commemorating the death of 2,000 Nisga'a after the volcano Wilksi Baxhl Mihl erupted in the 1700s. *Gary Fiegehen photo*

A surreal landscape, the lava fields of the central Nass Valley glow with a purple hue. Nisga'a Highway bisects the lava fields in the central valley. *Gary Fiegehen photo*

August 1775 the Spanish ship *Sonora*, with Lieutenant Juan Francisco de la Bodega y Quadra in command, lay in Chatham Sound, more than 100 kilometres to the west. There, according to the priest on board, Quadra's crew "suffered from the heat...which they attributed to the great flames which issued from four or five mouths of a volcano and at night-time lit up the whole district, rendering everything visible."

The two largest Nisga'a villages are located in the lava beds area: Gitwinksihlkw (Canyon City) against the northern wall of Nass canyon and to the east the capital, Gitlakdamiks (New Aiyansh), with its commanding view of the purple-hued lava rocks. Approximately 2,000 people live within these two settlements. Here, on the lee side of the Coast Mountains, the climate is sub-alpine, drier and colder than the coast, with an average winter temperature of about 3°C and summers averaging 18°C. Precipitation, often as heavy

Aerial view of Gitwinksihlkw. *Gary Fiegehen photo*

snowfall, averages 109 cm annually. The composition of the forests overlooking the villages has shifted from the hemlock, cedar and Sitka spruce of the lower river area to boreal spruce, lodgepole pine and balsam, though stands of cotton-wood still line the valley floor. At higher elevations mountain hemlock and sub-alpine fir predominate.

In the upper reaches of the Nass, north of these settle-ments, the river runs between the Coast Mountains and the Skeena Mountains. Thirty kilometres from Gitlakdamiks, beyond the Cranberry Junction rapids, lies glacier-fed Meziadin Lake. In this rich and remote habitat for moose and grizzly bear, the trees of the boreal forests, despite their natural anti-freeze, can shatter in the bitter cold of winter, with temperatures routinely falling to -50°C. The river then bends northeastward cutting through the Skeena Range, then north to its source in Magoonhl Lisims (Nass Lake). Just over the divide to the east lies the source of the Skeena;

Community Hall at Gitlakdamiks.
Gary Fiegehen photo

to the north lie two of the tributaries of the Stikine. Here
alpine forests give way to treeless mountain peaks. Of this
whole watershed, only the land near the river's mouth could
be remotely described as agricultural land.

Nisga'a elders contend that their people have lived in the
valley of the Nass since time immemorial, but until the last
quarter of the twentieth century, anthropologists were convinced that none of the aboriginal people of the Americas
had made their way from Asia over the Bering land bridge
more than 12,000 years earlier, each new wave of migrants
pushing earlier comers farther and farther south. The
Nisga'a, according to this theory, would be comparatively
recent arrivals, "naive foragers" who lived in small, mobile
groups with few possessions and little or no concept of property. These and similar anthropological speculations are

Nass Lake, the headwaters of the Nass River, near
the northern border of Nisga'a territory.
Gary Fiegehen photo

adamantly rejected by Nisga'a leaders such as Joseph Gosnell, who brusquely sweeps them aside as "the mistaken armchair speculations of the visiting professors."

However, new discoveries of tools and human remains suggest that the peopling of the Americas was much more complicated than just a few people walking across the Bering Strait. It appears likely that some also arrived by boat and that east Asian migrants may have been accompanied by Europeans. It is now also believed that the first migrants came at least 25,000 years ago. As well, recent research by the eminent anthropologist Wayne Suttles indicates that many centuries before contact with Europeans the early Nisga'a were living in large permanent villages and towns with an elaborate and complex material culture of ownership and control of property and monumental architecture. Their population densities were among the highest in pre-modern North America, irrespective of economy, with towns and villages ranging in size from a few score to more than a thousand individuals. As to who they are, ethnologists now classify the Nisga'a as members of the Tsimshian language group, which also includes the Gitksan Wet'suwet'en and other tribal groups from Prince Rupert south to Bella Coola. But the Nisga'a, Tsimshian and Gitksan languages are mutually unintelligible, and etymologists have yet to agree on the origin of the Nisga'a name.

The question then becomes why and how did Nisga'a civilization become so sophisticated without agriculture, the cornerstone of most other settled and civilized societies around the world? The answer has much to do with salmon and cedar—the two resources that became the building blocks of a remarkable maritime economy. All five species of Pacific salmon spawn in the Nass River: chinook first; then

Nisga'a chief, his family, his regalia and other
prized possessions at Gitlakdamiks, ca 1903.
RBCM 4330

Salmon drying, Nass River, ca 1906. *RBCM 6257*

sockeye, pinks (or humpbacks) and dog salmon; and last of all, coho. Pre-contact Nisga'a practised a highly efficient exploitation of this resource, catching the fish in nets made from stinging nettle fibre. They knew which species were to be eaten right away, and which were to be smoked and dried for winter. Sockeye and chinook, for example, could be utilized immediately or dried and kept for a short period, but it was only the dog salmon and coho which, when dried, could be stored throughout the whole winter. These dried fish, along with eulachon grease, became the staples in an extremely lucrative commerce with aboriginal peoples in the interior.

Cedar provided the Nisga'a with the material to make dugout canoes and houses. Their giant canoes allowed them to move frequently during the year, making temporary settlements near fishing or hunting grounds, shellfish beds or berry patches. The Nisga'a, however, were not nomads. They used the same seasonal stations each year and they erected either permanent houses or house frames that could be covered over with cedar planks brought along for that purpose. Their main residences were in the villages of the central valley, and they returned to them in winter when heavy seas slammed against the coast. These permanent homes, impressive ninety-foot-long structures made of logs and roofed with planks, reflected the basic Nisga'a social unit of the "house" or *wilp*—a matrilinear grouping that included several households and carried the name of its most prestigious chief. Depending on the number of related persons within it, a wilp could own one or several buildings in front of which were raised cedar totem poles intricately carved to represent the wilp's crest.

The wealth of the Nisga'a allowed the development of a highly complicated social and economic structure and complex rules of conduct. The people were organized into four clans: Gisk'aast (Killer Whale), Laxgibuu (Wolf), Ganada (Raven) and Laxsgiik (Eagle), then further divided into three classes: chiefs, commoners and slaves. Chiefs of high rank had vast authoritarian powers; lower ranking members were serf-like. Still, even mature society members of the lower classes were allowed to voice their opinions on group affairs as they held

Totem poles at Gitlakdamiks, ca 1901.
RBCM 4098 23

interest in group properties. Chiefs generally refrained from abusing those of the lower classes because, not only were they kin, but they provided the human capital for building or repairing houses, constructing fish weirs and traps, and paddling the huge dugout canoes. In addition, singers, dancers and attendants were needed for important ceremonies, and warriors were required to defend the group's wealth against invaders. The social structure was flexible enough, however, to allow low-ranking members to abandon chiefs who abused their power. It was a different story for slaves who, often captured in childhood, may have been treated well or ill, or perhaps traded or killed on an owner's whim.

Since the Nisga'a had no written language, their intricate social system and the rules for the apportionment of resources were embodied in a complicated oral code called the *Auuykhl Nisga'a*. As well, elaborate rites and ceremonies were used to establish responsibilities and ownerships, the most important of them

Nisga'a chief, ca 1928. *RBCM 4402*

being the potlatch, a word derived from the Chinook language, the lingua franca of the Northwest Coast. The potlatch was a feast, theatrical performance, gift-giving and confirmation ceremony. Status was formally and publicly assumed at one of these gatherings because, though place within the community was hereditary, it was not automatically assumed at birth. Potlatch guests served as witnesses to the bestowal of noble titles, crests and ceremonial rights. In return, they were given gifts according to rank, the more splendid going to those with the highest rank. In addition to the announcement of honours and titles, children of low-rank group members were awarded names and, sometimes, minor prerogatives.

Nisga'a culture emphasized the teaching of etiquette and moral standards, and all older relatives, particularly grandparents, participated in the education of children, much of it in the form of folk tales—amusing and entertaining, but

Modern-day Nisga'a feast, during which the women
of the hosting clan may feed as many as 500
people. *Gary Fiegehen photo*

always with a moral. Instruction began in infancy, at an age modern educators would consider too young to learn effectively. Children of status learned not only routine etiquette but also the lengthy traditions of rank and privilege, including the songs and prayers that denoted ownership.

All of these ritualistic aspects of the culture encouraged the development of distinctive art forms, and cedar wood became the basic raw material for the creation of masks and rattles for ceremonial use as well as more mundane objects such as boxes, storage chests, cradles, seats, bowls, spoons and other household items. All were carved and painted with bold designs, then trimmed with cedar bark fibres, shells, mountain goat bone or animal teeth. These designs represented family and clan crests; others depicted scenes from legends which, as the Nisga'a were essentially animist in their

Cultural historian Chester Moore and his grandson explore ancient petroglyphs in a rock outcrop in the middle of the Nass River, upriver from Gitwinksihlkw. *Gary Fiegehen photo* beliefs, told of the spirits or *halayts* of the sky, mountains, glaciers and animals. For the Nisga'a every living thing and natural element had a soul and a purpose and deserved respect. The legends were seamlessly interwoven with oral history because boundaries between human and animal, light and dark, were transitory and ephemeral, and supernatural beings such as the raven could change form and shape. As well, shamans enlisted the spirits to foresee the future, heal the sick, exorcize evil spirits, control the weather and bring success in fishing or hunting.

The disruption of this sophisticated culture and traditional lifestyle began with the arrival of Europeans on the Northwest Coast at the end of the eighteenth century. Probably the first white men to make contact with the Nisga'a were Russians who had been lured to the Northwest Coast after Vitus Bering's 1741 expedition to Alaskan waters had revealed an abundance of sea otters. The Russian fur traders who followed Bering concentrated on collecting pelts in the Aleutian Islands, then as the otter numbers declined around 1800, they began to look farther east and south,

Top: Carving tools.
Bottom: Carver Alver Tait preparing the Bear Den pole which was erected in 1992 in front of the community centre at Gitwinksihlkw. *Gary Fiegehen photo*

coming in contact with the Tsimshian people in the Stikine area and probably with the Nisga'a as well.

A British presence was established in April 1831 when a Hudson's Bay factory was constructed by Aemilius Simpson and Peter Ogden at the mouth of the Nass, near the modern village of Gingolx, and christened Fort Simpson. The British traders were struck by the fierce independence of the local people, but for all their fears, the expected hostility did not arise. Instead, the Nisga'a acted as middlemen, controlling the movement of furs from the interior to the coast and the trading post. This favoured position allowed them to obtain new metal implements—axes, knives, traps and firearms—but their ascendancy was not to last because the fort was abandoned three years later and re-established in Tsimshian territory.

Soon after contact with Europeans, a series of lethal epidemics swept through the Nass River Valley, decimating the Nisga'a population. While exact figures are impossible to prove, the Nisga'a estimate that between 1835 and 1906 diseases reduced their population by 50 percent. Demographic studies obtained by the Smithsonian Institute indicate that after 1775 every third person succumbed to smallpox. The first recorded epidemic to hit this area arrived in 1801; in 1824 the whole of the North Coast, including the Nass Valley, was ravaged by something known only as "the mortality." Smallpox returned again in 1836, measles in 1848, smallpox again in 1851 and 1862; these last two epidemics are estimated to have killed 43 percent of the Nisga'a who survived the earlier onslaughts.

The nature of the fur trade, in which the traders depended entirely on the First Nations to provide the pelts, coupled with the daunting size of many of the aboriginal groups, had ensured that the fur traders treated them more or less as equals, even while they saw them as inferiors. This was not true of the missionaries who followed them. For centuries, the conviction that Christians had a divine call to convert the world had animated believers to mount national and personal crusades and fuel them with their prayers, their fortunes, even their lives. This conviction gained new strength in the nineteenth century, as missionaries spread across the globe in ever larger numbers.

The first to come to the North Coast was the Anglican missionary William Duncan, who in 1862 established a "Christian village" at Metlakatla for his Tsimshian converts. There he demanded that his parishioners give up their clans and ranking system as well as dancing, shamanism and potlatching, and that they send their children to school and build individual family homes. His success in enforcing his rules was partially the result of a fortuitously timed smallpox epidemic which swept through Fort Simpson, killing one-third of the Tsimshian population. Duncan's converts, who were spared because of their isolation in the new settlement, were allowed to believe that this was the will of God.

Once successful at Metlakatla, Duncan encouraged a young colleague named Robert Doolan to go to the Nass Valley in 1864 to bring Christianity to the Nisga'a. Doolan established a mission near present-day Lakalzap, but he

Anglican missionary William Duncan.
BC Archives A-01175

made few converts, partly because he was competing with whiskey traders who anchored at the mouth of the Nass. In 1867 Duncan sent Robert Tomlinson, a medical missionary, to join him. Tomlinson was impatient "to overthrow dark superstition and plant instead Christian truths," thereby transforming the Nisga'a "from ignorant, bloodthirsty, cruel savages into quiet, useful subjects for our gracious Queen." Instead of continuing the attempt to gain converts near the Nisga'a's pagan villages, the two churchmen decided to follow Duncan's example and establish a new settlement free of hostile influences. Tomlinson masterminded the exodus of about fifty Christian sympathizers who set up a new village, which they called Gingolx (Kincolith), near the mouth of the Nass. Unfortunately, it was close to the eulachon grounds and friction soon developed with the Tsimshian who were used to camping nearby during the fishing season. The village reeled from crisis to crisis, and Tomlinson, realizing that his mission would never prosper as long as the bulk of Nisga'a

Metlakatla, ca 1870. *BC Archives 55798*

society remained pagan, set out in 1870 to found new Christian outposts in the central Nass Valley. The trip was marred when he inadvertently set fire to the trees near the river bank destroying, in his words, "an immense number of wild fruit trees, the berries of which are esteemed as a delicacy. A large portion of this land belonged to one of the chiefs, who thereupon fell into a temper with me, before he had even asked me whether I would pay for the mischief." On his next upriver visit, the chief whose trees had gone up in flames used his influence to keep the people from Tomlinson's services. Though the cleric was better received in other villages, the aboriginal attitude did not go beyond the norms of curiosity and politeness. He was greeted more warmly in a trip during the winter of 1874, but he was not successful in making a significant number of converts.

Another of Duncan's young acolytes was William Henry Collison, a schoolteacher from County Cork, who was dispatched in 1884 to Gingolx. Collison was responsible for the

Kincolith, 1881. *Edward Dossetter, American Museum of Natural History 42315*

rebuilding of the church there, after the original was destroyed by fire in 1891. Working alongside his wife Marion, a nurse, Collison lived among the Nisga'a until his death in 1922. The spire of his church still towers over Gingolx.

In Gitlakdamiks (Aiyansh), the most northerly settlement, the Anglican missionary James McCullagh, who arrived in the late 1880s, saw his job as taking "cognizance of one's parishioners—their domestic life, their dwellings, their sanitary arrangements, their civic life, their laws, government, etc.— as well as their souls." His goal was, in fact, the complete

Missionary William Collison attending to one of his flock. While he and the other churchmen taught many Nisga'a to read and write, he also despoiled and mocked their cosmology and spirituality. *RBCM 13181*

reconstruction of Nisga'a society. He
set up a parish council to short-cir-
cuit the network of the clan system
and substituted municipal and economic values for the economy of the
potlatch system. His mutual societies
included a fire insurance company, a
YMCA and YWCA, as well as a
"Harmonic Silver Band." On the economic side, too, his achievements
were impressive: a sawmill, a small
printing press, a dispensary, roads,

boardwalks, and some single-family cottages. According to
visitors, by the end of the century Gitlakdamiks was a rather
pretty village and, like Duncan's Metlakatla, the
Gitlakdamiks community became a model for travelling
Europeans.

The Methodists were represented by Alfred Green who
arrived on September 10, 1877, near present-day
Gitwinksihlkw. Within a year a school had been built and
Green began teaching the children to read and write, but it

Top: Churchman James McCullagh in his office in
Aiyansh. *RBCM 13186*
Bottom: Old Aiyansh, ca 1914. *RBCM 13096*

was ten years before the Methodist mission had enough parishioners and funds to build a church. Green's real contribution to life in the Nass Valley, however, was not in the form of religion. On a trip to England in 1881, he collected sixteen musical instruments and returned to start a brass band. With a month's intensive coaching, the Nisga'a made great strides, and Green reported joyfully that their repertoire included a half-dozen hymns and "God save the Queen." To this day brass bands are popular in the villages of the Nass River. After Green was transferred to southern British Columbia in 1889, the Methodist Church found it impossible to provide a replacement. Four successive Methodist ministers went to the village of Lakalzap—the Reverends D. Jemmings, R.B. Beavis, S.S. Osterhout and Dr. William Rush—but by 1900 that mission was also unable to attract any more candidates. Finally, in 1904, after four years without a minister, the parishioners asked the Anglicans to take care of them.

Aiyansh Brass Band. *RBCM 4196*

Anglican or Methodist, all of the missionaries to the Nisga'a were adamant that the heathen culture be swept away and replaced by Christian mores, but Green, Doolan and Tomlinson all complained of the strength of Nisga'a tradition. "It is strange to see," Green wrote, "how determined these heathen are to get the Christians back to heathenism. If they cannot get them by persecution they will try them by force, or by kindness work on their feelings." Collison was consumed with saving the souls of those who offended the Christian God with their shamanistic objects, but he collected many of the masks and rattles they gave up and sold them to traders who found a ready market for them in museums around the world.

These nineteenth-century churchmen left behind a complicated and painful legacy in the Nass Valley. On the whole, they were very successful at what sociologists describe as "directed culture change," teaching not only the Christian cosmology and basic reading and writing in the English language but a host of related social conventions, such as hygiene and etiquette, which they felt the Nisga'a people needed to know in order to participate in modern society. But from the start they misunderstood much about the

Nisga'a culture, viewing sacred totem poles and other objects as evil and in direct competition with the Christian cross.

Harry Nyce with artifacts being returned to the Nisga'a by the Archbishop of Caledonia in Victoria. *Gary Fiegehen photo*

They also misunderstood shamanism and believed that some shamans had the power to cause infirmities as well as to cure them. In their view the potlatch encouraged idleness, licentiousness and sloth, coercing the Nisga'a to give away their great wealth, which white society thought should be invested in economically productive ways, and slowing their progress toward civilization. The missionaries were successful in convincing the federal government that it was a pernicious institution and it was banned entirely through an amendment to the *Indian Act* in 1884. The missionaries' assaults added up to a kind of pincer-type attack on the core values of the Nisga'a, systematically destroying language, spiritual beliefs, customs, family structure and art, and leading many Nisga'a to reject their traditional culture.

Ironically, it was also the missionaries who helped organize the Nisga'a to promote their land claims and who wrote the endless Nisga'a petitions and protests to unsympathetic colonial officials, although it was the Nisga'a themselves who would drive the struggle in the end. As a result, the church has remained an important element of life in the Nass Valley. Many contemporary Nisga'a leaders are enthusiastic lay readers. Joseph Gosnell, Rod Robinson and Edmond Wright sometimes deliver Sunday sermons at churches along the Nass River. Clearly, they do not perceive the church as a destructive and oppressive force in their culture. Indeed, the church remains a vibrant centre of village life, and Anglican

Nisga'a leader Rod Robinson at the pulpit during a multi-denominational church gathering in Victoria.
Gary Fiegehen photo

services today incorporate aspects of traditional Nisga'a beliefs in hybrid services, sombre and touching, animated by a feeling of authentic spirituality. Robinson explains that he sees no contradiction between ancient Nisga'a beliefs and contemporary Christianity, pointing to parallels between the Bible and the *Ayuukhl Nisga'a* and drawing spiritual strength from both. It is the ancient oral code, however, that defines his Nisga'a name, his crest and his clan.

By far the most damaging aspect of European influence on Nisga'a life was the disruption of the economy of the Nass Valley. After Europeans had come to the coast, eulachon became an important commercial fish, but processors who set up fish-oil plants on the Nass River in 1877 soon found that the Nisga'a used so many of the fish themselves that there weren't enough left for a profitable export business. However, around the turn of the century the fishing companies again moved in on the Nass, and this time a thriving industry producing fresh, salted and smoked fish kept eulachon in fifth place among the coast's fisheries until 1912, when competition from other smelt fisheries around the world pushed eulachons out of the world markets.

Salmon canning began first on the Fraser River in 1867; in 1881 the first cannery had been established in Nisga'a country. The Nass River Cannery was soon followed by others: Arrandale, Nass Harbour, Portland, Pacific Northern, Mill Bay, Port Nelson, Cascade, Kumeon, Kincolith, North Pacific, and many smaller ones. By 1902, along the coastline between the Nass and the Skeena, there were thirty-eight canneries competing for fish to keep their operations going and, with chaos looming, the canners created BC Packers, an umbrella organization that oversaw the merging and rationalization of many of these companies. Each cannery had its

own fleet of rowed fishing boats that used gillnets to work the lower reaches of the rivers, and for the first few years on the Nass most of the fishers were Nisga'a and Tsimshian people. However, in 1878 the Canadian government decided to interfere with aboriginal fishing rights by introducing an initial restriction: a ban on the use of nets in the fresh waters of British Columbia. This regulation, badly designed for local conditions, was poorly enforced, but it was the first in a series of bureaucratic attacks on the aboriginal peoples' economic independence. In the same year, the federal fisheries department made a new distinction between food and commercial fishing, which effectively prohibited aboriginal fishermen from selling any fish caught by traditional methods to the canneries.

A further distinction between aboriginal and commercial fisheries was embodied in 1888 in a federal regulation that said: "Fishing by means of nets or other apparatus without leases or licenses from the Minister of Marine and Fisheries is prohibited in all waters of the Province of British Columbia.

Gillnet fleet at Mill Bay Cannery, ca 1921.
RBCM 17374

Provided always that Indians shall, at all times, have liberty to fish for the purpose of providing food for themselves, but not for sale, barter, or traffic, by any means other than with drift nets or spearing." This ruling completely ignored the fact that First Nations had always bartered fish and, from the beginning of the nineteenth century, had supplied white settlers with smoked and fresh salmon. Since aboriginal fishermen were now confined to a food fishery, by 1889 the federal government had effectively excluded them from all commercial fishing, and on the Nass Japanese and white fishers took the place of the Tsimshians and Nisga'as.

By the close of the nineteenth century, the ancient Nisga'a economy was in disarray. Divested of most of their lands and excluded from the fishing industry, and forced to become more and more dependent upon white American and British-Canadian manufactured goods, they scrambled to develop new economic patterns. By this time the fur trade was inconsequential, while logging and mining were still underdeveloped and required skills the Nisga'a did not have. Paradoxically, it was the fishing industry, which had so effectively deprived them of their fishing economy by monopolizing salmon streams, that now offered them entry into the foreign industrial economy. The canneries required literally thousands of workers from March, when the cans were manufactured, until September, when the last salmon run was over. And though they hired both aboriginal and Asian workers— mostly women—the cannery owners and their investors preferred aboriginal labour because it was cheaper than Chinese or Japanese as it did not have to be imported. Thus, over time the Nisga'a began to enter the new economic system, working for wages in a dull day-after-day routine, something that most other North American First Nations refused to do.

However, much of the Nisga'a world had been shattered. Rain-washed totem poles tilting into the salal marked the ruins of once-great houses, and the complex fabric of songs, stories, legends and myths that had given shape and structure to aboriginal society had been torn by recurring epidemics. Since the coming of the Europeans, the number of Nisga'a villages had dwindled from sixteen to four; from a population of perhaps 10,000, they now numbered about 700. Many Nisga'a had become nomads in their own land, but on one principle they remained adamant: they still refused to accept the ethnocentric assumptions of land ownership.

C H A P T E R   T H R E E :

The Great Land Grab

S ince colonial times, BC's aboriginal groups such as
the Nisga'a have had a consistent view of what their
pre-existing rights and titles were and from whence
those rights derive. In addition to the rights inherent
in their traditional forms of governance and law, aboriginal
groups point to the Royal Proclamation of 1763, in which the
British Crown explicitly recognized the existence and con-
tinuation of aboriginal title in British North America and
implicitly acknowledged the existence and continuity of aboriginal self-government. The *British North America Act* of
1867 made the Canadian federal government responsible for

The Nisga'a fought to shut down the molybdenum
mine at Kitsault, which they said was polluting
Alice Arm. *Gary Fiegehen photo*

the welfare of aboriginal people, but it was the 1876 *Indian Act*, a classic colonial document, that defined who was an "Indian," laid down a framework for a limited form of local government, outlined federal responsibilities for trusteeship of aboriginal lands and funds, exempted aboriginal peoples from taxes and generally set the terms and conditions of their existence. For example, unless they left the reserves and severed ties to their communities, they were not allowed to vote, a tactic that reflected the widespread belief within governments that assimilation into mainstream society should be the ultimate objective for aboriginal people. Indian agents were empowered to administer the *Act* throughout the country, their powers eclipsing those of traditional aboriginal leaders.

In short, the reserves were seen by agents and government policy-makers in Ottawa as way stations for aboriginal people pending their complete assimilation into mainstream Canadian society. As Sir John A. Macdonald said in 1880, using words that inspired federal thinking for a century, the government policy toward First Nations was designed to "wean them by slow degrees from their nomadic habits, which have become almost an instinct, and by slow degrees absorb them on the land. Meanwhile, they must be fairly protected." At best, the *Indian Act* reflected paternalism; at worst, it inflicted soul-destroying indignities.

Israel Powell, the Provincial Commissioner of Indian Affairs, ca 1874. *BC Archives F-03704*

In BC, however, colonial authorities generally conducted themselves as though aboriginal rights did not exist or had been extinguished with the advent of colonial and later provincial governments. In fact, in 1870 the colony of BC had unilaterally denied the existence of aboriginal title, claiming that the Nisga'a and other aboriginal peoples were too primitive to understand the concept of land ownership. This rationalization, appended to the then dominant myth that British Columbia was an empty land, was all that was needed to form the philosophical underpinning for the largest alienation of property—an area half the size of Europe—in imperial history. Sanctioned by Lieutenant Governor Joseph Trutch, the white settlers began a systematic land grab.

It was, therefore, all over but the mopping up by the time Provincial Land Commissioner Peter O'Reilly arrived at Gingolx on October 7, 1881, to spend thirteen days explaining the great land grab to the Nisga'a. He told them that once the territory had been surveyed and the Nisga'a allotted their reserve lands, "the government gives notice that the land outside the reserves may be purchased by white men." Later, O'Reilly told Premier Smithe that he had paid no attention at all to what the Nisga'a had to say about their traditional lands. He complained, "Every inlet is claimed by someone, and were I to include all these, it would virtually declare the whole country a

Peter O'Reilly (ca 1862), provincial surveyor who laid out Nisga'a reserves during the 1880s. The Nisga'a complained bitterly that the O'Reilly allocations created more problems than they solved. *BC Archives G-01065*

reserve." His method had been simply to identify the locations of dwellings and add to these a few fishing spots along the main watercourses.

In 1885, three Nisga'a chiefs travelled to Ottawa to meet with Prime Minister John A. Macdonald in an attempt to settle the land question and protest the amendment to the federal *Indian Act* of the previous year, which had outlawed cultural and religious ceremonies such as the potlatch— the major social, economic and political institution of the Nisga'a. They appealed to the honour of the Crown and cited the Royal Proclamation of October 1763, in which continuity of their land title had been specifically recognized, but they were rebuffed. A year later a group of white surveyors arrived at the mouth of the Nass to begin mapping out the Nisga'a reserve. They were met by Chief Israel Sgat'iin of Gitlakdamiks, dressed in a full-length grizzly bear cape and flanked by a group of fierce Nisga'a warriors. When he learned why the surveyors were there, the chief growled and imperiously ordered the surveyors to leave. They left, but others—backed by the military—soon returned to signal the imposition of reserves and boundaries for the administration of resource extraction. Chief Sgat'iin raged at O'Reilly and his system of reserves:

Old surveyor's transom, possibly the type used by O'Reilly and his crew. *Gary Fiegehen photo*

Chief Israel Sgat'iin in a robe of silver-tipped grizzly
bear. In 1886 he ordered provincial surveyors off
Nisga'a land. *Nisga'a Archives*

My heart is very sick because the white man want to take our land away from us, and do not make a strong promise to us on paper. We want a treaty, and want the government to give us something for our land. God gave us the land, and we picked our berries, got our furs, made our houses, and made our canoes; all our living came off this land, and out of this water, and now our hearts are made sick by the white chief's taking nearly all our land from us. We do not want a reserve if we do not have a treaty, for the reserve is not large enough for us to live on. Our berries and hunting grounds are not in the reserves. Mr. O'Reilly did not do right; when he was here he said he would take away my power and give it to another man. Mr. O'Reilly did not make me chief of Gitlakdamiks; my power came from my forefathers, and all in the village acknowledge that I am their chief, but because I did not want our land surveyed he said he would take my power away and give it to someone else. God gave us a good survey when he gave us the land, and we do not want Mr. O'Reilly to survey the land unless the government make a treaty with us, and give us a present for our land.

In 1887 Chief David MacKay told federal officials:

What we don't like about the Government is their saying this: "We will give you this much land." How can they give it when it is our own? We cannot understand it. They have never bought it from us or our forefathers. They have never fought and conquered our people and taken the land in that way, and yet

they say now that they will give us so much land, our
own land. These chiefs [of ours] do not talk foolishly,
they know the land is their own; our forefathers for
generations and generations past had their own hunting grounds, their salmon streams, and places where
they got berries; it has always been so.

In November 1888, Chief Tat-ca-kaks of Lakalzap raised his
eloquent objection:

I wish to say that every mountain and every stream
has its name in our language, and every piece of country here is known by the name our forefathers gave
them. And we are not satisfied with Mr. O'Reilly coming and measuring off our land. We do not understand
how he comes to get this power to cut up our land
without our being willing. When Mr. O'Reilly came
we told him how much land we wanted, but he would
not do what we asked. God gave this land to our

First Nisga'a Land Committee, ca 1883.
RBCM PN23037

fathers a long time ago, and they made gardens and made homes, and when they died they gave them to us. And strange Indians of other tribes who came here, wanting to fish the "oolichans," always asked our fathers for the privilege to come and fish here and always paid something for it. So this shows that all recognize that this belonged to us, and we have never been willing that our land should be surveyed.

Nisga'a leaders travelled in 1906 and 1909 to London to present their demands to King Edward VII, but he refused to meet with them. In 1910 and again in 1911, they travelled to Ottawa to meet with Prime Minister Wilfrid Laurier, who considered federal action to bring BC's provincial government to court for its failure to acknowledge aboriginal land claims. However, there was a provincial statute in place that precluded bringing an action against the province for an interest in the land without first obtaining an enabling document, called a fiat, from the province's Attorney General. This meant that any party wanting to sue the provincial government on such matters had to get the government's consent, and BC Premier Richard McBride refused to issue a fiat to the federal government. The Nisga'a then hired a firm of London solicitors to petition the king, to no avail.

After the defeat of Laurier's Liberal government in 1911 they formed the Nisga'a Land Committee to embark on their next efforts. At a meeting held in Gingolx in 1913, they adopted a "Statement of the Nisga'a Nation or Tribe of Indians" that reaffirmed tribal ownership of their traditional territory with all its natural resources, including fisheries. Though they cited George III's proclamation and other documents in favour of their claim, the Nisga'a based their position on a

principle that went beyond political authority, the principle of fundamental human rights:

> While we claim the right to be compensated for those portions of our territory which we may agree to surrender, we claim as even more important the right to reserve other portions permanently for our own use and benefit, and beyond doubt the portions which we would desire so the reserve would include much of the land which has been sold by the Province. We are not opposed to the coming of the white people into our territory, provided this be carried out justly and in accordance with the British principles embodied in the Royal Proclamation. If therefore as we expect the aboriginal rights which we claim should be established by the decisions of His Majesty's Privy Council, we would be prepared to take a moderate and reasonable position.

Nisga'a Land Committee, ca 1913.
Nisga'a Archives

Convinced an appeal to Westminster would work in their favour, the Nisga'a hired the London law firm of Fox and Preece, and on May 21, 1913, their petition was brought before the Privy Council. However, the Privy Council had no jurisdiction to consider the matter as that body was only responsible for hearing appeals referred to it by the Canadian government.

Meanwhile, back in Canada, Duncan Campbell Scott, deputy minister of Indian Affairs, was having none of it, and for the next ten years he dodged determined aboriginal land claimants, still convinced that the "Indian Problem" would vanish as assimilation became complete. To this end, in 1920 all aboriginal children in Canada were ordered to attend white schools, to be run for the most part by the churches. Prior to this time, in addition to the small village schools operated by church missions, an informal system of off-reserve "industrial schools" had existed as a co-operative effort between church and state, with the federal government subsidizing church efforts through a series of financial grants. Under the new law, the churches set up formal boarding schools, known generally as residential schools, in which they were expected to teach all the basics of a white education and specifically discourage aboriginal culture and language. Under this system, most of the Nisga'a children were sent either to Coqualeetza Residential School at Sardis in the Fraser Valley or to St. Michael's Residential School at Alert Bay on Cormorant Island, near Port Hardy. Both were run by the Anglican Church.

In 1924 the government of British Columbia finally allotted the Nisga'a people 76 square kilometres of reserve land, less than one percent of the 25,000 square kilometres they had claimed as their territory. This allotment represented approximately one-tenth of a square kilometre for each Nisga'a man, woman and child. Had they been farmers on the rich alluvial lands of the Fraser River delta, they might have made a living; but the Nisga'a were hunters and fishers and the land they were assigned consisted of steep rock formations and lava beds in a climate not conducive to agriculture.

But there were small victories during this time: in 1923 aboriginal peoples were granted the right to hold commercial ocean-fishing licences. However, to Scott's surprise, this was not enough to stop their determined efforts to obtain a treaty and resolve their land claims. As a result, in 1927 he drafted an amendment to the *Indian Act* to "discountenance" land claim agitation once and for all. His amendment was specifically designed to prohibit the Nisga'a and all other other aboriginal groups from hiring lawyers to assist in settling land claims. It included this paragraph:

> Every person who, without the consent of the Superintendent General expressed in writing, receives, obtains, solicits or requests from any Indian any payment or contribution for the purpose of raising a fund or providing money for the prosecution of any claim which the tribe or band of Indians to which such Indian belongs, or of which he is a member, has or is represented to have for the recovery of any claim or money for the benefit of the said tribe or band, shall be guilty of an offence and liable upon summary conviction for each such offence to a penalty not exceeding two hundred dollars and not less than fifty dollars or to imprisonment for a term not exceeding two months.

Although apparently only denying aboriginal groups the assistance of lawyers, Ottawa had in effect also prohibited them from organizing and meeting to discuss land claims because no one could provide them with money to travel, and no one could rent them a hall in which to meet. As a consequence, aboriginal activists went underground for a long period of hibernation, from 1927 until the repeal of the law in 1951—a period later described by Joseph Gosnell as a "time of darkness and despair for all aboriginal people." However, ignoring federal laws, the gentleman outlaws of the Nisga'a Land Committee met secretly to keep alive their dream for a resolution of the land question.

The federal government's amendments to the *Indian Act* in 1951 removed not only the prohibition against funding land claims but also the law against potlatching. In Victoria, although the government still refused to countenance land claims by the aboriginal communities, the legislature had removed all restrictions on voting privileges in 1947. Both federally and provincially the motivations for these changes had less to do with fairness to the aboriginal peoples than with governments' need to polish up this country's international image. In any case, both governments generally assumed that these long prohibitions of rights had had the desired effect: that the First Nations had given up on their claims of aboriginal title, that they had forgotten their quaint traditional customs, and that they were ready now to be assimilated into the body politic and be good Canadian citizens like everybody else in the county. They were wrong.

CHAPTER FOUR:

The Peaceful Warriors

o the best and brightest of Nisga'a leaders, the settling of the land question has always been the holy grail, central to Nass River political life for more than 150 years, and in the early 1950s two remarkable men emerged to focus their attention on treaty making. The first was Frank Calder, a diminutive, revving engine of a man. The other was Joseph Gosnell's older brother, James Gosnell, a firebrand for aboriginal rights.

Frank Calder was the visionary for change in the Nisga'a's world. His life had begun at the edge of myth. In 1915, the former leader of the Nisga'a Land Committee,

---

Peaceful warrior Edmond Wright.
Gary Fiegehen photo

Chief Na-qua-oon [Long-Arm]—Arthur Calder—had lost his infant son while travelling on the Nass River. Shortly afterwards, an elderly woman had a vision and announced that Mrs. Calder's younger sister was pregnant with the reincarnated boy. The male child, born on August 3, 1915, was handed over by his natural parents and adopted by the chief as Frank Calder. "In 1919, when I was four years old," Frank Calder relates,

> Arthur Calder took me to Gingolx into Walter Haldane's house, where all the leading chiefs were going to talk land claims . . . Jeffrey Benson, who died not too long ago . . . was the young man who was doing the secretarial work at the meeting . . . Arthur Calder picked me up and stood me on the table and said to the gathering: and this is the boy I am going to send to a white area, and I'm going to make him speak like a white man, I'm going to make him walk like a white man, I'm going to make him eat like a white man. Everything that man does, this little boy is going to do. We don't need interpreters. By the time he is ready, he is the boy that's going to be using our language, his language, and he is the one that's going to bring this case to the highest court in the land.

As early as age nine, young Calder was invited to take part in the activities of the land committee. "The books were placed in my hands on this," he says. To give him a white man's education his parents sent him to the Coqualeetza Residential School near Chilliwack, where he spent thirteen years. He went on to the University of British Columbia as the first status Indian ever admitted to that institution, and he graduated

from the Anglican Theological College with a licentiate in
1946. His student days gave him splendid opportunities to
learn from the experience of aboriginal leaders and particularly Squamish leader Andrew Paull, whom Calder calls his
"tutor." Deciding against ordination, Calder plunged into the
world of politics and spent his next few years in the provincial
legislature as a champion of aboriginal equality in areas as
diverse as pensions, citizenship, trapping, fishing, and medical and social services. His moral status among the Nisga'a
soared when, in 1958, he became one of their most important
hereditary chiefs, assuming the title of Chief Na-qua-oon

Frank Calder with radio reporter Jack Webster
in a Vancouver studio, 1967.
National Film Board of Canada

from his natural father, Henry Clark, who had succeeded Arthur Calder to the title since he had died without the traditional nephew to come after him.

In October 1955 Calder resurrected the old Nisga'a Land Committee but re-fashioned it as the Nisga'a Tribal Council. Though he became its president and chief spokesman, it was the backing of the very influential James Gosnell that helped to convince all four clans and villages to join the organization. Revered in Nisga'a villages today, James Gosnell was known as "Jimmy" to his contemporaries, although the affectionate diminutive hardly fit the imposing figure of the man who looked opponents right in the eye and dared them to contradict him. His kinetic energy was captured in black and white by an early 1960s National Film Board crew. A riveting orator whose voice could roar with outrage, he was also a determined strategist. As far as aboriginal title is concerned, he declared:

> We are the true owners of British Columbia. The Indians across the province own everything—the rivers, the trees, the bugs, the animals. You name it. Subsurface rights, the air, the rain, the whole shot. That's what we mean when we say we have aboriginal title to the land ... But whoever said we are seeking ownership of all of BC? Never has that been said. We are willing to share, and have said so thousands of times. Aboriginal title is the starting point for negotiations. Exclusive ownership of BC will obviously not be the end point of the negotiations. We want an agreement that will fairly recognize your laws and systems of government, and in return you will recognize ours.

Nine years younger than Frank Calder, James Gosnell had also attended the residential school at Coqualeetza, but his time there had been short and he had been happy to return to village life and become a fisherman like his father, a hereditary chief of the Eagle Clan. It was in the wheelhouse of his father's gillnetter that he became inspired to settle the land question, and by 1946, at age twenty-two, he was embroiled in Nisga'a politics, serving a fourteen-year term as chief councillor at Gitlakdamiks. In 1946 he married Christine Adams and together they raised fourteen children; all six of their sons became fishermen like their father, who was happiest out on the salmon and halibut grounds. A skilled skipper, he provided not only for his immediate family but often for the whole village, sharing a whole truckload of salmon, halibut and shellfish. "He loved fishing," his daughter Bonita Gosnell recently recalled, but after he became embroiled in resolving the land question, he spent much of his time in meetings, exhorting his colleagues to action. Even as a young girl Bonita was well aware of the electric effect her father's oratory had on the villagers: "When he spoke, people listened." Calder agrees. "Jimmy was a very aggressive personality; the case had to move and Jimmy was the man to make it move."

James Gosnell liked to tell media people that the Nisga'a and other aboriginal peoples owned the province "lock, stock and barrel." When this was reported, it frightened some people and hardened critics who warned of dire consequences if the governments gave in on land claims. But Gosnell also preached that the Nisga'a themselves must be fair. In 1983, in a speech to an aboriginal group in Ontario, he exhorted the Nisga'a and all other aboriginal peoples to "be responsible for themselves" before he unleashed a blistering fusillade against intransigent governments in Ottawa and Victoria that had treated the Nisga'a like "monkeys in a cage."

Nobody cares about you and me. Nobody! Don't kid yourself. It's you and me only. That's all. And we can do it. We can do it because our grandfathers did it way before the white men came.

They're not doing a damn thing for our people, and I'm sure everyone of you are the same way. That is the reason why we're proposing self-government, to create employment for our people in the forest industry, in the commercial fishing business, tourism, mining. Right now nobody's doing anything for us. Nobody.

Who should be responsible for us? I don't trust anybody. I'm talking about white men. I don't even trust the priests. We should be responsible for ourselves, that's what self-government is all about, to be responsible for yourself.

The federal government hasn't done a damn good job for us. The provincial government isn't doing a damn thing for us. Nobody gives a hoot about you or me. Let's not kid ourselves. That's why we are proposing an Indian self-government, to govern ourselves. We governed ourselves way before the white man came to this land. Our rulers were our chiefs, we call them hereditary chiefs today. They were the law and order in those days. We owned sections of land where I come from, no doubt it's the same way here, I don't know whose land this is, but everything you needed to survive is in the land. That's what they took away from us. That's why we are the way we are today.

We're like a bunch of monkeys in the cage. They're called Indian Reservations, that's where you and me are in today. That's where they put us. They expect us to survive in the cage.

I'm not happy with welfare. My grandfathers were never on welfare. Everything that we needed was on the land. It's the resources of the land that they're taking today that belongs to you and me. But we're on welfare.

James Gosnell, the Nisga'a firebrand who rallied his people in the struggle for aboriginal rights.
Ralph Bower/Vancouver Sun, *1982*

What's this self-government? Do we hear "another third order of government?" You're damn tootin' we're proposing a third order of government. They just expect us to live like monkeys in a cage. They give us a couple of peanuts every now and then to live on while they themselves are living like kings.

We do not have a say in the commercial fishing industry on the coast where I come from. In the timber, the best timber in the world, we don't have a say in that. Today we're 95 percent unemployed in my territory, the provincial government couldn't do a bloody thing about it, nor is the federal government. That's why we're proposing self-government. We want to manage those trees, we want to manage the salmon, we want to have a say in the mining that's now going to go on in our area, because we want a piece of the pie, and we want to have a say in a piece of the action in which decisions are made. That's what self-government is all about.

We're the true owners of this land of ours. That's what gets me so bloody fed up and I'm not going to quit and I won't trust anybody. Never trust anybody, because nobody has been good to us, you and me. Nobody. And that's why we should have self-government.

They want to erase us forever, that's why. You better believe it. But they're not going to erase my name forever.

The Nisga'a Tribal Council was more effective than the Land Committee had been, partly because it was an organization of all the Nisga'a people rather than just an organization of the leaders, as the Committee had been. But its main drive came from Calder's politically sophisticated leadership, and under his direction it soon became a strike force for treaty making. The starting point for the next major stage of the Nisga'a's political evolution came in 1963 after a court case on Vancouver Island caught Calder's attention. Two Nanaimo aboriginal men named White and Bob had been arrested for killing six deer on Crown land. Their lawyer, a young social activist named Thomas Berger, obtained an acquittal. At the core of his argument was an 1854 document signed by Governor James Douglas that recognized the aboriginal ancestral hunting rights. Judge Swencisky of the County Court ruled that this document was indeed a treaty, and that "the aboriginal right of the Nanaimo Indian tribes to hunt on unoccupied land, which is confirmed to them by the royal proclamation of 1763, has never been abrogated or extinguished and was still in full force and effect." This ruling was later upheld by the Appeal Court of British Columbia.

Regina v. White and Bob was to have ramifications far beyond the demise of a half-dozen Vancouver Island deer because Calder and his tribal council colleague Rod Robinson, frustrated with government intransigence, had been searching for a lawyer who "understood the concerns of Indian people." Within weeks, Calder and Berger embarked on the most significant human rights cases in Canadian history—to prove the Nisga'a had retained aboriginal title and rights. The Nisga'a action began on September 27, 1967, before the Supreme Court of British Columbia. In their statement of claim, they asked the court to issue "a declaration that the aboriginal title (also known as Indian title) of the Plaintiffs to their ancient tribal territory has never been

Thomas Berger, 1977. *Brian Kent*/Vancouver Sun

lawfully extinguished." The Nisga'a claimed their title by virtue of the Royal Proclamation of October 1763 or, if not, by other imperial legislation, since "no part of the said territory was ever ceded to or purchased by Great Britain or the United Kingdom and no part of the said territory was ever ceded to or purchased by the Colony of British Columbia." This being the case, the Nisga'a argued, BC's land legislation was invalid. The "Calder Case," as it became known, went to trial in April 1969 before Mr. Justice Gould. As president of the tribal council, Frank Calder was one of the first witnesses called by Berger. Part of the transcript follows:

Q: Do you know if the Indian people who are members of the four Indian bands on the Nass River regard themselves as members of the Nisga'a tribe?

A: Yes, they do.

Q: Apart from their language, do they share anything else in common?

A: Besides the language, they share our whole way of life.

Q: Now, Mr. Calder, I am showing you exhibit 2, which is a map Mr. Brown [the province's lawyer] and I have agreed upon. Does the territory outlined in the map constitute the ancient territory of the Nisga'a people?

A: Yes, it does.

Q: Have the Nisga'a people ever signed any document or treaty surrendering their aboriginal title to the territory outlined in the map, exhibit 2?

A: The Nisga'a have not signed any treaty or any document that would indicate extinguishment of the title.

Q: Can you tell his lordship whether the Nisga'a today make use of the lands and waters outlined in the map, exhibit 2?

A: Put it this way, in answer to your question, from time immemorial the Nisga'a have used the Nass River and all its tributaries within the boundaries so submitted, the lands in Observatory Inlet, the lands in Portland Canal, and part of Portland Inlet. We still hunt within those lands and fish in the waters,

Frank Calder (front centre), flanked by his colleagues, gets set to present the legal case to BC Supreme Court, 1967. *Nisga'a Archives* streams, and rivers, we still do, as in time past, have our campsites in these areas and we go there periodically, seasonally, according to the game and the fishing season, and we still maintain these sites and as far as we know, they have been there as far back as we can remember.

We still roam these territories, we still pitch our homes there whenever it is required according to our livelihood, and we use the land as in time past, we bury our dead within the territory so defined and we still exercise the privilege of free men within the territory so defined.

Berger later called Professor Wilson Duff, the eminent British Columbia anthropologist who explained traditional Nisga'a relationship to their land. When asked if the aboriginal community at large recognized the Nisga'a's title to the Nass Valley, he explained:

All of the surrounding tribes knew the Nisga'a as the homogenous group of Indians occupying the area delineated on the map. They knew of them collectively under the term Nisga'a. They knew that they spoke their own dialect, that they occupied and were owners of that territory and they respected these tribal boundaries of the territory.

Q: Now, are you able to tell the court whether the Nisga'a tribe made use of the land and the waters delineated on the map beyond the limits of the reserve that appear on this map in the McKenna-McBride report?

A: Yes.

Q: Is there any significance to the location of the reserves on the Portland Canal and Observatory Inlet and the Nass River?

A: Yes, I think I can say that in many cases these small reserves were located, for example, on the Portland Canal at the mouth of the tributary stream, at the mouth of a valley. The reserve is a small piece of land at the mouth of the stream which, to a degree, protects the Indian fishing rights to the stream.

Q: Now, prior to the establishment of these reserves, what use would the Indian people have made of the areas which flow into the mouths of the streams and rivers?

A: The general pattern in these cases would be that the ownership of the mouth of the stream and the seasonal villages, or habitations that were built there, signify the ownership and use of the entire valley. It would be used as a fishing site itself and a fishing site on the river, but in addition to that, the people who made use of this area would have the right to go up the valley for berry picking up on the slopes, for hunting and trapping in the valley and up the forest

Eminent anthropologist Wilson Duff, 1949.
RBCM 16430

slopes, usually for hunting of mountain goats. In other words, they made use, more or less intensive use of the entire valley rather than just the point at the mouth of the stream.

Q: Can you tell his lordship the extent of the use to which the Nisga'a have put the lands and waters in the area delineated on exhibit 2 [the claim area] and how intensive that use was?

A: This could be quite a long statement.

Q: Well, I think we can live with it.

A: And much of it has already been said. However, the territories in general were recognized by the people themselves and by other tribes as the territory of the Nisga'a tribe. Certain of these territories were used in common for certain purposes, for example, obtaining of logs and timber for houses, and canoes, totem poles, and the other parts of the culture that were made of wood, like dishes and the boxes and masks, and a great variety of other things, and the obtainment of bark, which was made into forms of cloth and mats and ceremonial gear. These would tend to be used in common. Other areas weren't tribal territories, would be allotted or owned by family groups of the tribe and these would be used, different parts, with different degrees of intensity. For example, the beaches where the shellfish were gathered would be intensively used. The salmon streams would be most intensively used, sometimes at different times of the year, because different kinds of salmon run at different times of the year. The lower parts of the valley where hunting and trapping were done would be intensively used, not just for food and the hides and skins and bone and horn material that was used by the Indian culture, but for furs and different kinds of large and small animals which were either used by the Indians or traded by them. The farther slopes up the valleys, many of them would be good

Mountain goats. *Gary Fiegehen photo*

mountain goat hunting areas. This was an important animal for hunting. Other slopes would be good places for trapping of marmots, the marmot being equally important, and there are a great number of lesser resources, things like minerals of certain kinds for tools and lichen and mosses. It becomes a very long list.

Q: Go ahead.

A: Now, in addition to this, the waterways were used for the hunting of sea animals as well as fishing of different kinds. They were used also as highways, routes of travel for trade amongst themselves and for their annual migration from winter to summer villages, and a great variety of minor resources from water, like shellfish of different kinds, fish eggs, herring eggs. There is a great list of such minor resources in addition.

Q: To what extent would the use and exploitation of the resources of the Nisga'a territory have extended in terms of that territory? Would it have extended only through a limited part of the territory or through the whole territory?

A: To a greater or lesser degree of intensity it would extend through the whole territory except for the most barren and inaccessible parts, which were not used or wanted by anyone. But the ownership of an entire drainage basin marked out by the mountain peaks would be recognized as resting within one or other groups of Nisga'a Indians and these boundaries, this ownership would be respected by others.

Later during the trial, Duff said that the Nisga'a had a precise notion of property and explained how ownership was orally documented through a system of kinship and hereditary chiefs.

It took the Supreme Court of British Columbia a month to reject the Nisga'a claim. Mr. Justice Gould ruled that the Nass Valley had been at the time of the Royal Proclamation *terra incognita*, but this fact alone would not be enough to deny the Nisga'a claim. That would depend on a definition of "aboriginal title," and since no definition existed, he ruled that any rights the Nisga'a might have had before contact had been extinguished by "overt acts of the Crown Imperial by way of proclamation, ordinance, and proclaimed statute." Undeterred, the Nisga'a quickly filed an appeal.

Meanwhile, as Calder and Berger had been working the case through the courts, the Liberals and their new leader, Pierre Elliott Trudeau, had been returned to power. By June 25, 1969 his government had prepared a White Paper called *Statement of the Government of Canada on Indian Policy* to present to Parliament, and in a speech in Vancouver on that same day he told his audience that "To be an Indian, is to lack power—the power to act as owner of your lands, the power to spend your own money and, too often, the power to change your own condition." The solution he proposed was to integrate the aboriginal people into Canadian society by opening "the doors of [equal] opportunity" to them and by bringing their special status to an end. Trudeau insisted that although the government would recognize existing treaty rights in the short run, it was "inconceivable that in a given society one section of society have a treaty with the other section of the society." In the long run, Indians "should become Canadians as all other Canadians." In Trudeau's vision for Canada, this country would belong to tomorrow's world, and he insisted that nothing was unchangeable but "the inherent and unalienable rights of man."

Trudeau's new "participatory democracy" was introduced to the aboriginal peoples of Canada by Jean Chrétien, the new minister in charge of the Department of Indian Affairs and Northern Development (DIAND). After the most extensive opinion-sampling poll ever undertaken by the federal government, his ministry had drawn up a set of alternatives published in the booklet *Choosing a Path*, which was given to every band council and aboriginal organization. They were given about six months to absorb the proposals, then meetings were arranged with aboriginal groups at Prince George, Terrace, Nanaimo, Kelowna, Chilliwack and the Yukon. For many aboriginal leaders, these were days of bright promise, as the struggle for aboriginal rights became evident to the general public. The *Vancouver Sun* and other newspapers began to investigate the issues on a regular basis, introducing the subject of aboriginal rights to a mass audience, and they documented complaints about the inadequacies of Indian Affairs aid and employment programs.

My father, *Sun* reporter Ron Rose, filed some of his stories from the Nass River. He recalls the excitement when some of the Nisga'a and other aboriginal leaders first saw their names in print. He also remembers being taken to task when some leaders—unwilling to accept the need for balance in reporting—strongly criticized him for including comments from critics. Two sessions in northern BC offered a study in contrast. "Some of the delegates at Prince George had never been to a city before, some hardly spoke any English," he recalls. "One old woman had walked miles through the bush and had to scare off a grizzly bear blocking her trail. In full-throated oratory, Chief Nick Prince told the assembly that Indian lives had been ruined by the white man, a theme that would ping pong across Canada for the next thirty years."

But to the newsmen present, the most surprising aspect of these sessions was that almost all of the submissions by the aboriginal leaders were professional, concise and written in university-level English—hardly the language of those who stood at the podium. The explanation for this lay in the fact that back in October 1968, to meet the rising expectations of aboriginal peoples, senior officials from the Department of Indian and Northern Affairs and a mysterious group of social activists known as the "animateurs" arrived on the West Coast. Their task was to set up a series of meetings with British Columbia and Yukon tribal groups in order to give them a greater voice in shaping future policy.

At the Terrace hearings, held in a ramshackle hotel at nearby Lakelse, my father, who had arrived a day early, met some of these animateurs, the advance guard for the committee. Their sole role was to give last-minute briefings to the aboriginal leaders on awkward issues they would bring before the committee. "They were hippie-type rabble-rousers and I had a wild evening with them and several of the aboriginal leaders at a roadhouse on the outskirts of Terrace. At the end of the evening I said to one of them, 'See you tomorrow,' and he laughed and said, 'Like hell you will. We'll be long gone. The committee doesn't want to know about us.' As I recall, there seemed to be a war within the Indian Affairs department. The bureaucrats, whose role it was to see that the caretaker function of what was then called the Department of Indian Affairs and Northern Development was carried out efficiently, were fighting off attacks from these social activists. I don't remember any of their names now, but I ran across one of them some years later in a high position on the Ottawa headquarters staff."

During the early 1970s, the social foment inspired by these activists was part of a general political awakening of aboriginal peoples across Canada increasingly dissatisfied with the conditions of their existence. They were being helped for the first time by non-aboriginal people, political science graduates and journalists in particular, who embraced this political cause and summoned the injustices of history to assist them. Some non-aboriginal supporters, lodged in university departments of Native studies or history or in niches of the country's media, so sympathized with aboriginal demands that they dropped scholarly inquiry to become advocates for the cause.

Those hearings were an eye-opener to anyone who cared to watch. My father said they changed his perception of the aboriginal people, and I, too, was affected. I remember him bringing home some of the tribal leaders he met and being surprised, as a middle-class youngster, at their warmth and scope of their understanding. It was my first realization that they were people and neighbours with whom we shared the province.

Trudeau's White Paper on Indian Policy—the very title was sneered at by aboriginal peoples as a white man's joke—had the unintended effect of clarifying visions and thereby polarizing discussion. And the handbook given out to aboriginal leaders, which had at first appeared to embody an even-handed philosophical debate, soon revealed itself as merely a tool for government theorists who were really aiming at equality for the aboriginal peoples through assimilation. Their framework for analyzing the aboriginal problems was universally condemned by aboriginal organizations that recognized it as

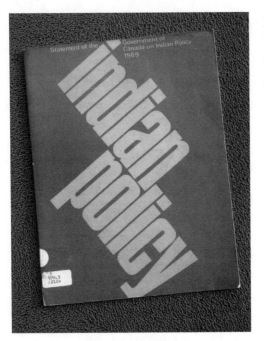

yet another attempt to assimilate them into mainstream Canadian society—a condemnation that had the rare virtue of being completely accurate. It was an echo of the three long-standing complaints that aboriginal peoples were already voicing: that the Confederation Settlement of 1867 had provided inadequate recognition of their rights; that it established a paternalistic regime in relation to them; and that it set in motion a campaign to systematically extinguish a way of life. Far from exciting aboriginal people with a new vision, Trudeau's vision sent them searching for an older one in a new guise, that of self-determination. Eventually Trudeau himself acknowledged the failure of his White Paper. "We had perhaps the prejudices of 'small l' liberals," he admitted. "That's why we said, Let's abolish the *Indian Act* and make Indians citizens of Canada like everyone else."

On October 30, 1969, DIAND Minister Jean Chrétien visited the Nass Valley to address the twelfth annual Nisga'a convention and open the new community centre at Gingolx. He told an expectant audience of Nisga'a people they had "the basic and fundamental right to be masters of their own future, to be responsible for what is theirs, to profit from what is theirs." The courts, however, were in the process of coming to an entirely different conclusion. In a unanimous decision in May 1970 the appeal court of British Columbia

Cover of the federal government's controversial White Paper, the "assimilationist" document fiercely rejected by the Nisga'a and other aboriginal organizations.

upheld Gould's ruling in the Calder Case. Chief Justice H.W. Davey of the BC Court of Appeal announced that the Nisga'a "were undoubtedly at the time of settlement a very primitive people with few of the institutions of civilized society, and none at all of our notions of private property. I am not overlooking Mr. Duff's evidence that the boundaries of the Nisga'a territory were well known to the tribes and to their neighbours, and respected by all. These were territorial, not proprietary, boundaries, and had no connection with notions of ownership of particular parcels of land."

Meanwhile, the Calder Case had encouraged other aboriginal groups to begin agitating again for settlement of their land claims, and in Ottawa there was a dawning realization that the problem was not going to go away. However, the BC Court of Appeal's decision on the Calder Case suddenly put a damper on the ardour of aboriginal organizations for immediate resolution of their claims, and when the Nisga'a, absolutely convinced of the moral rightness of their cause, prepared to appeal to the Supreme Court of Canada, the leaders of other aboriginal peoples argued against it. If the Nisga'a lost, it was obvious to them that their own claims could go nowhere. But the Nisga'a went ahead with their appeal, and in November 1971 the chiefs of the four villages in the Nass Valley, together with village elders wearing their traditional sashes, travelled to Ottawa for the hearing of their case in the Supreme Court of Canada. For five days, seven judges heard the argument of the appeal. Then they reserved their decision for fourteen months.

The judges were divided in their ruling. Mr. Justice Wilfred Judson, speaking for three judges, found that the Nisga'a, before the coming of the white man, had aboriginal title, a title recognized under English law. Enlarging on the nature of Indian title, he said, "The fact is that when the settlers came, the Indians were there, organized in societies and occupying the land as their forefathers had done for centuries. This is what Indian title means. What they are asserting in this action is that they had a right to continue to live on their lands as their forefathers had lived and that this right has never been lawfully extinguished." Having said this, he then determined that such title had been effectively extinguished by the old pre-Confederation colony of British Columbia.

Mr. Justice Emmett Hall, speaking for three judges, found that the Nisga'a, before the coming of the white man, had aboriginal title, that it had never been lawfully extinguished, and that this title could be asserted even today. He said,

Frank Calder meeting Prime Minister Trudeau and Indian Affairs Minister Jean Chrétien in Ottawa, 1973, soon after the Supreme Court of Canada handed down its historic split decision. *Nisga'a Archives*

"What emerges from the . . . evidence is that the Nishgas [the common spelling at the time] in fact are and were from time immemorial a distinctive cultural entity with concepts of ownership indigenous to their culture and capable of articulation under the common law, having developed their cultures to higher peaks in many respects than in any other part of the continent north of Mexico." He held that the Nisga'a title could be asserted today, no matter that the province would be faced with innumerable legal tangles. What was right was right.

The seventh judge dismissed the case on a technicality but did not address the question of aboriginal title, so on the main aspect of the case—whether the Nisga'a had retained title to the land—the court was tied. What was significant for aboriginal rights was that all of the six judges who had addressed the question supported the view that English law, in force in British Columbia when colonization began, had recognized aboriginal title to the land.

Berger, commenting later on the Supreme Court's judgement, said that although it was not handed down until February 1973, it had come at a politically auspicious moment. The election of 1972 had returned the Liberals to power under Trudeau, but as a minority government. To remain in office, the Liberals would have to depend on the goodwill of the opposition parties, so the question of aboriginal title was catapulted into the political arena. Both the Conservatives and the New Democrats insisted that the federal government must recognize its obligation to settle aboriginal claims. The all-party Standing Committee on Indian and Northern Affairs passed a motion that approved the principle that a settlement of aboriginal claims should be made in regions where treaties had not already extinguished

aboriginal title, and on August 8, 1973, Minister of Indian Affairs Jean Chrétien announced that the federal government intended to settle the claims. On January 12, 1976, the Nisga'a Tribal Council formally opened negotiations with representatives of the federal and provincial governments in a ceremony at Gitlakdamiks, though it was not until 1990 that the province actually joined the talks.

But it was not Frank Calder who would lead the Nisga'a into these negotiations. Throughout this period, his political career had been in turmoil. In 1972 when Dave Barrett and the NDP swept to victory in British Columbia, Calder, as the NDP member for Atlin, had joined the Cabinet as minister without portfolio, the first aboriginal cabinet minister in Canadian history. His job was to make recommendations to the government on relations between the aboriginal peoples and the province; nobody seems to have told the new premier

First tripartite meeting on the Nisga'a land claim, held January 12, 1976. *Nisga'a Archives* that this was the same man who had sued the province in the Nisga'a case—a classic case of conflict of interest. But apparently Barrett did not fire Calder from Cabinet until an incident in July 1973, which involved drinking, a woman and a car parked in the middle of an intersection. While Calder denied the allegation, the story embarrassed the Nisga'a, and at the Tribal Council's next annual convention in 1974, James Gosnell defeated Calder in the election for president. Calder quit the NDP and ran in the 1975 election as one of Bill Bennett's Social Credit can-

didates. Re-elected, he returned to the legislature to sit once more on the government side, but he was defeated by a single vote in 1979 as the riding swung back to the NDP. He retired from politics that year.

It was therefore James Gosnell who led the Nisga'a when they sat down with federal negotiators in January 1976. However, in the early 1980s he was diagnosed with cancer, and he died in August 1988 in a Prince Rupert hospital after a lengthy illness. The land question had taken most of the last thirty years of his life, and as he lay dying in the palliative care ward, he apologized to each of his children for being an absent father. To a *Vancouver Sun* reporter who came to see him he gave a message to convey to British Columbians. "If the BC government figures that Jimmy Gosnell is going to die, and so goes the land claim, they're badly mistaken, badly

Frank Calder, 1972. *The* Province

mistaken," he said. "It's going to come. There's no question in my mind. It has to come. But maybe I will be visiting with St. Peter when that day comes." Sitting beside his dying brother, Joseph Gosnell knew that the job was now his to complete.

A weary James Gosnell in 1985, three years before his untimely death. Vancouver Sun

Joseph Gosnell was given new ammunition with two court decisions of the 1990s. The groundwork for a broad interpretation of aboriginal rights over natural resources was laid in 1990 by the case known as *Regina v. Sparrow*, which began when Ronald Sparrow, a Musqueam, was charged with contravening regulations by fishing in the lower Fraser River with a driftnet longer than that permitted by Department of Fisheries regulations. Sparrow's appeal from his conviction in the lower court was based on the argument that the restriction on the net length was invalid because it was inconsistent with Section 35 of the *Constitution Act* of 1982, a section that recognizes and affirms existing aboriginal and treaty rights.

The Sparrow Case was the first in which the Supreme Court of Canada had been called on to interpret what Section 35 actually means. In overturning Sparrow's conviction, the court ruled that the *Constitution Act* provides "a strong measure of protection" for aboriginal rights and that any proposed regulations that infringe on the exercise of those rights must be justified. More specifically, the court ruled that aboriginal and treaty rights are capable of evolving over time and must be interpreted in a generous and liberal manner; that governments may regulate existing aboriginal rights only for a compelling and substantial objective such as the conservation and management of the resource; and that after conservation goals are met, aboriginal people must be given priority to fish for food, social and ceremonial purposes.

By its decision in the Sparrow Case, the Supreme Court of Canada gave the Nisga'a legal ammunition to have their fair share of the Nass River fisheries written into their treaty. The Delgamuukw Decision, on the other hand, gave greater weight to Nisga'a oral history in their deliberations with the government. Delgamuukw involved the Gitksan and Wet'suwet'en people, whose hereditary chiefs sued the provincial and federal governments in 1984 over ownership of and jurisdiction over 58,000 square kilometres of their traditional territory east of the Nass Valley. The case derived its name from that of one of the traditional chiefs who initiated the claim. The trial before the BC Supreme Court lasted from May 11, 1987 to June 30, 1990, but it was not until March 8, 1991 that Chief Justice Allan McEachern dismissed the chiefs' claim in a controversial decision based on his flat rejection of the use of oral history as evidence. In 1993 the BC Court of Appeal also dismissed the claim for jurisdiction but did acknowledge that the Gitksan and Wet'suwet'en had "unextinguished non-exclusive aboriginal rights other than the right to ownership" and said that these should be negotiated with government.

The case then went forward to the Supreme Court of Canada, and in December 1997 that court opened the door to the acceptance of aboriginal oral history as evidence, contradicting Judge McEachern's decision, and it encouraged the two sides to seek a negotiated settlement outside the courts. The decision raised the expectations of some aboriginal groups and had an immediate effect on ongoing BC land claims cases as well as contributing to a new wave of aboriginal militancy in other parts of the country. But here again, the Nisga'a stood apart. After carefully reviewing an impartial legal assessment of Delgamuukw, Gosnell and his colleagues determined there was little reason to change course and pressed on to ratify the treaty they had negotiated.

CHAPTER FIVE:

The Consultants

or those who choose to visit Indian Country, or have it suddenly thrust upon them, no passport is necessary. In British Columbia, a drive down a gravel road, a boat journey up an unnamed fiord, or a visit to the landlord's office on Southwest Marine Drive just outside the Vancouver city limits will get you there. The fact is, the whole of British Columbia is Indian Country, even though the aboriginal peoples are invisible to many. They are the unemployed neighbours few of us talk about, the troubled child at the school, the Indian chief with the brand new Ford Explorer, the victims on the nightly news. Like an uncle in the basement, they have lived here forever—and they aren't going away. And while they comprise just 3 percent of Canada's population, in northwest communities such as

Consultants and negotiators. *Gary Fiegehen photo*

Terrace and Prince Rupert, they represent up to 25 percent of the total population, and their numbers are growing fast.

There is one group in this country, however, that is fully aware of the aboriginal presence. In towns and cities across the province, they are known as the "Indian industry": the legion of lawyers, consultants, foresters, geographers, biologists and public relations men hired to help steer the clunky machinery of the treaty negotiations process—always, of course, in concert with their aboriginal clients.

With their eyes fixed on the prize of a treaty, the sharp-minded leadership of the Nisga'a Tribal Council had realized from the day they first hired lawyer Thomas Berger that they would need white lawyers and consultants to help in their struggle, and in the early 1970s they began headhunting for talent in the same way corporations do. Geographers or tax consultants, for example, would be brought in to provide a particular service or piece of information needed to back up the Nisga'a's case, just as they would be hired by a corporation planning a new initiative. Of course, applicants for jobs with the Tribal Council were measured by certain criteria: the Nisga'a preferred lawyers and consultants who were sympathetic with their world view. Implicitly at least, those they hired were expected to understand and believe in the Nisga'a struggle against injustice, so there was a kind of natural selection at work here.

Thomas Berger, 1983. *Ian Lindsay*/Vancouver Sun

White consultants working on the
Nisga'a's core treaty-making team
included the principals of the
Vancouver law firm of Rosenbloom
& Aldridge, who worked out of
offices on the thirteenth floor of the
Marine Building. Jim Aldridge acted
as lead counsel and architect of the
treaty. But over the years as the various iterations of the treaty were put
to paper, Aldridge and Don
Rosenbloom and the members of
their firm worked with lawyers from
other firms as well—specialists in tax
law, fiscal relations and forestry regulations. Also, lawyer-activist Thomas Berger, who had
worked earlier with Frank Calder, returned in the late 1990s
to help fight anti-treaty court challenges by Gordon
Campbell and the BC Liberal Party. Other technical consultants hired by the Nisga'a included a geologist, a forester, a
tourism expert and two fisheries biologists from a firm in
Sidney, BC. During the 1970s a sociologist had also been
hired to interview elders and write down for the first time the
Ayuukhl Nisga'a, the ancient oral code of conduct. In the
1990s a legal expert who helped frame the South African
Constitution under Nelson Mandela was hired.

I was hired by the tribal council to write background materials and help create a positive public environment for the
treaty and, as the debate intensified, to implement a quick-
response system that could get the Nisga'a message out to
the media to counteract the blitzkreig of anti-treaty commentary. My work and that of my colleague, Bob Spence, a

Thomas Berger (left) and Jim Aldridge at the
Law Courts. *Gary Fiegehen photo*

Nisga'a communications consultant Bob Spence
and elder Dorothy Doolan. *Gary Fiegehen photo*

former host of CBC radio's *Early Edition*, was directed by Nisga'a communications coordinator Eric Grandison. Together we developed a strategy of "soft" public education—books, speeches, opinion page articles, brochures, videos and a Web site—to build support and understanding for the treaty. However, as the battle for public support intensified, we helped Joseph Gosnell and the Nisga'a team shift to a program of hardball media tactics that continued right through the countdown to treaty ratification. Through it all, Gosnell's high-road presentation and on-camera dignity was critical to our success.

We were all paid on a fee-for-service basis, with the lawyers receiving a substantial share. And while the total cost for this small army of white consultants over the decades remains confidential, it is reasonable to estimate that the aggregate figure comprises a not insignificant portion of the $51.3 million it cost the Nisga'a to finalize the deal during the twenty-three-year period. But the largest portion of this money—a loan which the Nisga'a must repay to the federal government—was paid out for per diem fees, accommodation, food and airfare for the Nisga'a negotiating team, plus office and secretarial services, long-distance fax and phone bills and related expenses.

Many of the white consultants who went to work for the Nisga'a were university educated, well versed in political science, the conflict theory and other tenets of social activism, and they genuinely felt their efforts would help the Nisga'a bring home a treaty. And for the most part, all the players of the "industry" were vigilantly attenuated to each and every nuance of the politically correct canon. But across the cultural divide, misunderstanding was common and could lead to comic results. On his first visit to the Nass River Valley, one public education specialist was greeted by a Nisga'a chief with: "Great. You can write speeches to make me sound like a white man." Another consultant, driving though a blizzard on the dangerous stretch of road between Terrace and Gitlakdamiks, pulled up to the Tribal Council office on time for a mid-morning meeting. He was met at the door by a senior Nisga'a chief—the only other person around—who thanked the consultant for his determination and explained that because of the snow, none of the other Nisga'a had made it in, and the meeting had been cancelled. Waiting for a plane at the Terrace airport, an environmentalist, dressed head-to-toe in Patagonia clothing was holding forth on the evils of logging practices when he was politely interrupted by a Nisga'a chief: "I logged as a young man. It was the best job I ever had. And once our treaty is ratified, we will once again be able to log in our own forests."

A few consultants were smug, unbearable pedants who bestrode a high and holy ground of some undefined utopian socialism. Wielding their ideology like a blunt axe, they projected their dreams on the Nisga'a and used aboriginal rights as a weapon in their crusade against capitalism and corporatism, seldom acknowledging they might be updating a time-honoured pattern of white cultural appropriation of aboriginal people and their traditional values. The quest for the Nisga'a Treaty allowed others to perpetuate their disdain of the ruling classes, of the so-called hypocrisy of business and government.

On the other end of the scale were the dreamer-consultants, the failed idealists and poets *manqué*, who worked with aboriginal groups as a salve against the crush of the commercial world. Doing well by doing good, they became part of a new family, seldom considering or admitting that an over-identification might not be in the best interest of their client. Some were "nice people" praising themselves for their vulnerability and finding distinction in their personal failure. Making the Nisga'a the objects of their enlightened interest, a few white consultants went on to make them the objects of their pity, then of their wisdom, ultimately of their coercion. On the back roads of Indian Country, the trail to a treaty was paved with good intentions.

Other consultants were social reformers driven by an enlightened notion of good works. In Victoria, Anglican parishioner Mavis Gillie was a tireless advocate for the Nisga'a cause for more than twenty-five years. On her own initiative, she wrote letters to the editor and prowled the halls of the legislature where, meeting and greeting politicians and their senior bureaucrats, she would hand out the latest public relations missive. A volunteer foot soldier in the Nisga'a struggle, she neither expected nor received financial

Long-time Nisga'a supporter Mavis Gillie greeted by Herbie Morven. *Gary Fiegehen photo*

remuneration for her efforts. Meanwhile on the political front, Jim Fulton lobbied hard for the Nisga'a during his fourteen years as the NDP MP for Skeena, turning his office on Parliament Hill into an informal command post and research centre for the Nisga'a negotiating team.

Over the years many churchmen had been staunch allies to the Nisga'a. Anglican priests such as Ian Mackenzie played important roles in the early days of the Nisga'a quest, and then came back in the 1980s and early '90s to develop public education strategies for raising awareness and fostering support for Nisga'a treaty making. Commuting from his home in Terrace to the tribal council office in Gitlakdamiks meant a ninety-minute drive on a treacherous road that would often ice over in winter. On three occasions he was literally driven off the road by logging trucks. A mysterious, heavy-set man, somewhat reminiscent of a Graham Greene character, he has a peculiar sense of humour and appeared to delight in tormenting other white consultants. Picking them up at their hotels, often after they'd spent the night drinking, Mackenzie would drive at top speeds north to the Nass, watching from the corner of his eye while his passengers gagged beside him. Letting out the clutch on the icy switchbacks at Lava Lake, he shared insider gossip about tribal bosses while chuckling at the discomfort of his prey.

In his youth, Mackenzie had helped to found the high-rise student housing co-operative and free university known as Rochdale College in Toronto and with others developed the first aboriginal-run, post-secondary educational institute in Canada. He later earned degrees from Union Theological Seminary in New York and the University of Kings College in Halifax. His work among BC's aboriginal populations began in 1974 in the Haida village of Old Masset, and he moved to the Nass in 1979 as rector at St. Andrew's Anglican Church in Lakalzap, where he was soon adopted into the Raven clan. The geographical isolation—this was in the years before the Lakalzap bridge was built—proved difficult for Mackenzie and his family, and not just because the river would ice up in winter, making for dangerous crossings. "Non-aboriginal people had to demonstrate they were not going to behave like white colonists," Mackenzie recalls. "Our three years in Lakalzap were sometimes tough for my children who had to go through a very difficult period of social adjustment. Some of the villagers were suspicious of whites, although I don't blame them for that." Curiously, Mackenzie's recollections parallel those of painter Emily Carr who, in her book *Klee Wyck*, takes a chapter to describe the suspicious stare of a Lakalzap woman. Impassive and above all, disapproving of everything she saw, including Carr, her face spoke of long isolation and an inconsolable despair.

Other consultants who came to the Nass Valley simply needed the

Anglican churchman Ian Mackenzie (top) and former MP (NDP-Skeena) Jim Fulton both actively supported Nisga'a treaty making.
Gary Fiegehen photos

work. Jim Skipp, a graphic designer from Vancouver, was hired to help design a program of public education materials to explain the treaty to the general public. He welcomed the work because it seemed like a project with more scope than an annual report or another standard piece of public relations—what he described as "pipe-bending brochures." He provided an honesty sometimes in short supply among these consultants by candidly admitting he had begun enjoying his Nisga'a consultancy more after he realized its significance.

Like all white consultants, Skipp would soon learn the realities of Indian Country the hard way. On his first Nisga'a assignment he stayed at Nass Camp, a series of interconnected trailers where loggers bunk down for the night. He was accompanied to the adjoining recreation hall by a Nisga'a chief who beat him at several games of pool, then the two of them retired to a booth to drink a few beers. Here they were joined by a ferociously drunk and angry unemployed Nisga'a welder who, it was soon made obvious, had little time for tribal council politics and even less for its Nisga'a bosses. Within minutes the welder, his barrel chest pumped for action, was looking for a fight. Trapped in an inside seat, Skipp had to use all his verbal skills to extricate himself and retire to the safety of his room. Next morning, he was awakened by the sound of running water. Standing at the sink in the common bathroom, an itinerant mushroom picker, cleaning up before another shift, was washing her breasts.

Vancouver graphic designer Jim Skipp with press proofs for *Nisga'a: People of the Nass River*. *Gary Fiegehen photo*

Gary Fiegehen, a Vancouver-based photographer who worked for the Nisga'a Tribal Council over a period of more than a decade, has his own story to tell. Hired to photograph the annual convention of the Nisga'a Tribal Council in Gitlakdamiks in 1990, during which Joe Gosnell was elected president, Fiegehen was perplexed by the Nisga'a's lack of response to a series of speeches delivered by federal and provincial ministers. Time and again, tribute was paid to the patience and determination of the Nisga'a, to the wisdom of the elders and the skills of the negotiators. In fulsome praise, the white politicians assured the assembly that governments in Ottawa and Victoria were committed to doing the right thing, to correcting the wrongs of the past, and to proceeding without further delay to finalize a treaty that would define a new and better day for the Nisga'a and all Canadians—*if only the Nisga'a could wait a little longer.* Trying to frame photographs in the dim light of the community hall, Fiegehen was moved by the rhetoric. At last, he thought to himself, a treaty was in the offing. But why, he wondered, was there no applause from the Nisga'a people, who sat like stones in their seats?

Over the years Fiegehen, who documented the people and places of the Nass River in a dazzling hardcover book, grew to understand. "This was the first but not the last moment of my disillusionment as visiting politicians came and went," he said. "There was no applause because the Nisga'a people had heard variations of the same speech over and over. Be patient, the people were told. Always be patient. You are a moderate, law-abiding people who trust in the honour of the Crown. All the while during this period of 'talk-and-log,' white fallers worked overtime to clear-cut the Nisga'a forests."

There were social activists on the aboriginal side of the debate as well, a brave and courageous few who fought alongside the Nisga'a. Confronting authority, they saw the Nisga'a quest as one of basic human rights. With the skills and talent to work for corporations and big-city law firms, they chose instead the drama and struggle of Nisga'a treaty making. At stake was a real community with a real history of suffering, struggle and persistence. Besides, all of the Nisga'a consultants took a quiet pride in engaging their powerful adversaries, countless legions of them. State-sanctioned, hefting notebook computers, the troops of the "Anti-Indian Industry" had instant access to corporate, government and editorial boardrooms. Staying in better hotels, wearing better clothes, their numbers dwarfed by several orders of magnitude the relative few who worked alongside the Nisga'a.

Nisga'a communications coordinator Eric Grandison (left) with consultants Sara Whitney and Gary Fiegehen during a Nisga'a art show held at the Canadian Museum of Civilization. *Gary Fiegehen photo*

One powerful critic was Thomas Flanagan, a professor of political science at the University of Calgary and former director of research for the Reform Party of Canada, who wrote the book *First Nations? Second Thoughts*. On a talk show to tout his book on Prince George's radio station CKPG on July 28, 2000, he admitted his role in the Indian Industry: "It has become an industry, and I don't know where it is going to end. And to be frank here, I make a nice bit of money on the side by working as a consultant for the Crown in land claims cases, historical testimony. I mean, it is good for me personally—extra income. And interesting work. But is it good for the country? I don't think so."

In his book Flanagan dissects what he calls the "prevailing orthodoxy" that determines public policy towards aboriginal peoples, arguing that this orthodoxy enriches and empowers a small elite of activists, politicians, administrators, middlemen, and well-connected entrepreneurs, while bringing further misery to the very people it is supposed to help. Canadian policy on aboriginal issues, he states, has come to be dominated by an ideology that sees aboriginal peoples as "nations" entitled to specific rights. The Nisga'a and other tribal groups now enjoy many legal privileges, including rights to self-government beyond federal and provincial jurisdiction, immunity from taxation, court decisions reopening treaty issues settled long ago, the right to hunt and fish without legal limits, and free housing, education, and medical care as well as other economic benefits. Underpinning these privileges is what Flanagan describes as aboriginal orthodoxy—a set of beliefs that hold that prior residence in North America is an entitlement to special treatment; that aboriginal peoples are part of sovereign nations endowed with an inherent right to self-government; that aboriginal people must have collective rather than individual property rights; that all treaties must be renegotiated on a "nation-to-nation" basis; and that aboriginal people should be encouraged to build prosperous "aboriginal economies" through money, land, and natural resources transferred from other Canadians.

Whenever the site of the treaty talks shifted to the small towns of Terrace or Prince Rupert, it was unavoidable that the consultants from the three sides would be thrown into each other's company. Walking the streets or having dinner at Don Diego's Mexican restaurant, those of us who worked for the Nisga'a team would meet our adversaries, the members of the federal and provincial teams. Although each side had its own agenda, over time all three parties shared the kind of camaraderie often seen among professional athletes who, although playing on opposing teams, speak the same language and often share a similar world view. Besides, nearly all the consultants were from middle-class backgrounds, and we were all getting a "real world" lesson in political science.

In late night off-duty sessions around the horseshoe bar of the Terrace Hotel, the consultants would compare their own mythologies, sorting out their feelings about the Nisga'a struggle. The math was easy enough: they were being paid to provide a service just as they would be with any other client or business. On the other hand, especially for those set up on long-term retainers, the landscape had become a more ragged and complicated place where contradictions and complexities pitted the ground, cloaking it in a fog of white, middle-class guilt. To begin with, by signing with the Nisga'a, no matter what their initial motivations, the consultants had identified themselves with a subgroup invisible to most Canadians: an impoverished, marginalized group of aboriginal people who

lived a village life where some seemed paralyzed by despair.
And because they worked with the Nisga'a, they became
known as "Indian lovers," an insult that shocked some into
the recognition that at its essence, the "Indian Question" in
this country has much to do with race, a subject rarely
acknowledged and often denied by many Canadians who
subscribe to the dominant mythology of Canada's
"Peaceable Kingdom." Some of us were even afforded a
glimpse of what it must be like to be an aboriginal person in
this country. During my ten years of working side by side
with the Nisga'a, racism ceased to be an intellectual con-
struct for me and became more a daily fact of life. I began to
understand that the racism in this country is far more complicated, far more subtle and far more insidious than appears

DIAND Minister Ron Irwin (left) and Harry Nyce
arrive at Gingolx for the 38th annual Nisga'a
convention, 1995. *Gary Fiegehen photo*

to be the case for African-Americans. On the streets of Terrace, Prince Rupert, or for that matter, throughout British Columbia, aboriginal people are too often treated as if they were invisible, the ghost at the crossroads, the apparition by the riverbank. Others dismiss them as if they were children. From my observation in the northern towns few whites were overtly racist. However, I know that the Nisga'a refused to stay at one particular Terrace hotel because of an unpleasant altercation with the management there many years ago. Other businessmen and women used coded language to patronize, demean and deride even while they were happy to do business with the Nisga'a.

Fortunately there was a good supply of humour from Gosnell and other Nisga'a leaders that helped to smooth the rough seas of cultural dissonances for the consultants. And when the Nisga'a hit the bar during those after-hours sessions at the Terrace Hotel—especially in the earlier days

Consultants from the three parties hammer out the wording for the Agreement in Principle, February, 1996. *Gary Fiegehen photo* when a bright promise hung in the air—many of the jokes they told about the white consultants were genuinely amusing. Gentle, inclusive and filled with a genuine decency, the Nisga'a would also poke fun at each other's weaknesses and acknowledged it was human to make mistakes. However, although drinking with the tribal bosses was important, there was always a sense of being on call, and as a result, newer consultants on their first trip "in country" would howl with exaggerated laughter at the chiefs' jokes.

Making sense of these contradictions meant more sessions at the bar, of course. Here Gary Fiegehen offered a perspective beyond his Nikon lens: inspired by Buddhist thought he would explain concepts of that ancient religion from Right Intention to hungry ghosts if he felt his comrades were serious in their inquiries. One night, after completing a photo assignment, he was perched on a favourite bar stool, rolling a cigarette and expanding on "disparaging speech" as one of

Marge Percival studies her notebook computer while Nelson Leeson bows his head in fatigue during the long negotiations. *Gary Fiegehen photo*

the hindrances to enlighten-ment. Bathed in the surreal blue light of the bar, he reminded us of Nisga'a nego-tiator Nelson Leeson's recent speech during which he said that without mutual respect there can be no trust, and without trust no treaty. Suddenly there was a rude interruption to his soothing exegesis: another white con-sultant arrived, commenting loudly on the lazy and lack-adaisical style of one Nisga'a leader. Fiegehen's riposte was sharp: "What right do you have to judge? You haven't lived his life."

None of us had. We had our own lives, which we seldom if ever referenced in the company of the Nisga'a bosses—the tough men who, forever poring over stacks of legal docu-ments, had to make so many hard-fought compromises about their land and culture during the long years of the campaign. But we consultants were snugly inside the Nisga'a canoe, and for a brief shining moment when the treaty was ratified, we would be able to bask in a reflected glory, always attendant to the Nisga'a chiefs.

Yet another meeting. Two decades of talking took its toll on the Nisga'a negotiating team.
Gary Fiegehen photo

CHAPTER SIX:

The Negotiators

T he Nisga'a people—law-abiding, moderate and, above all, committed to a negotiated settlement— stand in stark contrast to those First Nations people of British Columbia who employ confrontational, quasi-military tactics to try to resolve their long-standing grievances with senior governments. Since the mid-1970s tensions between these militant groups and government agencies has steadily escalated, and after the aboriginal Warriors Society's clash with police and the army at Oka, Quebec, in 1990, confrontations here began erupting into violence. Five years after Oka, at Gustafsen Lake in the Cariboo, an armed standoff between an eccentric group of aboriginal sundancers and RCMP officers lasted for weeks,

Chateau Granville Hotel, home away from home
for the Nisga'a for more than twenty years.
Courtesy Best Western Chateau Granville

and created a frenzy of media coverage. By comparison, smaller incidents, such as roadblocks across access roads to resource sites, seem almost routine. During the summer of 1995 alone, there were roadblocks at Pavilion, Pemberton, Penticton, Moricetown, Oliver, Alert Bay and Agassiz, all generally related to disagreements over land use and ownership, all covered by the media.

For *Vancouver Sun* aboriginal affairs reporter Terry Glavin there were two ways to get a story. Often braving bad weather, he could fly to the nearest airport and rent a vehicle with oversized tires to navigate the rough back roads. If he was lucky, he might eventually find himself huddled against a rusty wood stove in a drafty Indian Affairs standard-issue house, sharing chewing tobacco with an old man who didn't speak English very well while he tried to discern what had caused the ruckus, roadblock, standoff or dispute in the first place.

During that period, Glavin also had another source. He would flag a cab to the Chateau Granville Hotel, one of the Best Western chain. It perches at the south end of

Vancouver's Granville Mall—a strip of nightclubs, peep shows and bars. Set off Helmcken Street at an absurd angle, the late-modern concrete box squats massive and bleak, its cheery pink awning unable to mitigate the effects of an almost Soviet-style functionalism. Was there ever a less chateau-like edifice? But the staff is friendly, the roof doesn't leak, and the rates are reasonable for a city of expensive rooms. Although it targets

Author Terry Glavin, a treaty supporter.
Gary Fiegehen photo

business travellers and tourists on a budget, by the mid-
1980s this hotel had also become the home-away-from-
home for the more upscale coastal tribes, as well as the
Native Brotherhood, the First Nations Congress and many
other aboriginal groups. It had thus become known as the
place where a certain aspect of the political culture of BC's
Indian Country found its urban roost—a clearing house of
information.

It was in the coffee shop of the Chateau Granville that
Glavin witnessed the parade of characters it was his job to
write about: the aboriginal leaders, the Howe Street suits and
their lawyers, the fishing company executives and their
lawyers, the mining company executives and their lawyers,
the Indian Affairs program administrators, the ministry
negotiators, the deputy ministers and assistant deputy ministers and directors and deputy directors and regional direc-
tors-general and program managers. And it was here that he
would interview the aboriginal leaders, some wearing $1,000
sea bear bracelets, some of them dressed in Armani suits,
though they didn't know how to read and hired lawyers to
help them do so. He talked to Indians with the shaky hands,
Indians who hid their smiles because of their bad teeth, alco-
holic nephews of the old men who huddled 1,000 kilometres
away around rusty wood stoves, the sons of once-proud fishing families whose boats now listed, rotting at the dock in
coves and harbours from Tsawwassen to Port Edward.
"These young men, the finest minds of their generation, got
hooked on airline reservations, hotel food, cellular tele-
phones, Jack Daniels, air-conditioning and $50 hookers and
meetings, more meetings, and more meetings," Glavin rue-
fully recalled in a later telephone interview. "And at the end
of the day, every day, week in and week out, they would

return to whatever solace they could find in the fetid and smoke-filled bar at the Chateau Granville Hotel."

The Nisga'a also stayed at the Chateau Granville, but they arrived packing notebook computers and their well-thumbed editions of *Robert's Rules of Order*. They came for a more prosaic purpose: to attend formal "tri-partite" land claims negotiations with the federal and provincial governments. For them, the Chateau Granville served as the Vancouver base for a series of meetings that would, to an outsider at least, appear to be an endless and farcical regime of scheduling. Because there were three parties involved—the Nisga'a, the federal government and the provincial government—it had been decided that meetings would rotate between the three jurisdictions. The federal government chose Vancouver as its base, scheduling meetings either in the Chateau Granville for the convenience of the Nisga'a or at the Department of Indian Affairs and Northern Development offices at the corner of Seymour and Georgia. The provincial government, of course, presided in Victoria, where the consultants stayed in Executive House; however, because of the high tourism occupancy rate in Victoria, it was often difficult to book meeting space there. The Nisga'a generally used Terrace for their meetings, with the negotiators staying at the Terrace Inn, but they also held court in Gitlakdamiks or in Prince Rupert, where many sessions were held at the Highliner.

Typically, the formal session would begin at 9 a.m. and continue until 5:30 or 6 p.m., but sometimes there were evening sessions as well. Teams often broke into smaller groups—lands, finance, fisheries, forest resources, economic development, self-government—and, as the treaty came nearer to completion, these groups would subdivide into five or six subgroups. The logistics of this meant adherence, at all costs, to a kind of quasi-military discipline, meted out by the negotiators themselves. Initially there were two-week breaks between sessions, but in later years, as the treaty neared finalization, the teams would work full-time, week after week, Monday through Thursday. On Friday, the Nisga'a would meet by themselves to review the week's work and make plans for the next phase. Then they would travel back home or on to the next city for the next round, forever circling from Terrace to Vancouver to Victoria to Prince Rupert and then back again.

Both Ottawa and Victoria had assembled powerful negotiating teams. The federal government operated with a core of seven to ten people, but their consulting specialists often sat at the table as well. The provincial team led by Jack Ebbels had a core of seven people, though that number sometimes rose to ten, as well. Both had a phalanx of experts to guide

DIAND Minister Jane Stewart and federal negotiator Tom Molloy during the historic signing of the Nisga'a Agreement in Principle in Gitlakdamiks on August 4, 1998. The event made front-page news around the world. *Gary Fiegehen photo*

them in areas such as forestry or fisheries. However, because of an enormous talent base, more resources and unlimited funding, the provinces and the feds could rotate key players and bring in new personnel, like professional sports teams. Unfortunately, many of these negotiators began their tours of duty with only the most general ideas of the issues they would have to confront during the protracted process. In the months leading up to the signing of the treaty, the federal government's lead negotiator, David Osborne, was replaced by Tom Molloy, known as "the closer." Only a short time earlier, Osborne's $300,000-plus annual contract had been disclosed in an article published by the *Vancouver Sun*, using facts gleaned under the *Freedom of Information Act*; this news caused much consternation among the negotiating lawyers on all three teams.

Over the years of negotiating, the membership of the Nisga'a team numbered as high as thirty because the Nisga'a insisted in making all their decisions in traditional consensual style and therefore felt it critical to include all their hereditary chiefs as well as elected tribal council politicians in the process. Most of the Nisga'a negotiators were married and had families, but for weeks, even months on end they were separated from them. Family lives became strained, spouses and children failed to comprehend why treaty making required missing so many school assemblies, teacher conferences and weekends at home. For the negotiators the endless hotel rooms and hotel food, little exercise and numbing days in negotiating sessions took an all too human toll. In the early years of the formal talks, several of the team wrestled with drinking problems exacerbated by lifestyle diseases such as diabetes and obesity. As the team members reached middle age, there were increasing health concerns and a pervasive sense of lost time. They grew greyer, balder and heavier. For many, exercise and hobbies had become things of the past. They lived in a kind of bubble, in an extraordinarily controlled, unnatural process.

But at least these men had jobs; they were being paid for their labour. Each member of the Nisga'a negotiating team received a per diem of at least $300 a day to sit on one or more of the committees. And while their counterparts with the federal and provincial teams earned substantially more, this remuneration was a princely sum considering how few jobs there were in the four Nisga'a villages, where an unemployment rate of 80 percent means a life of seasonal work and welfare. But more important than the money for the negotiators, treaty making was a holy grail, and the members of the team were willing to sacrifice themselves—and their families—in order to bring home a deal.

But it was a long and bumpy ride. First, the Nisga'a had to negotiate a framework agreement with Victoria, eventually signing it in 1991. A provincial election in 1991 disrupted the talks and, once back at the table, the newly elected NDP government had to formulate policies to direct its negotiators. A federal election in October 1993, during which the federal Liberals under Chrétien routed the Tories, resulted in the federal negotiators having to re-adjust their negotiating machinery to fit with the dictums of the federal Liberal's Red Book. Then BC's policies were adjusted again when Glen Clark took over from Mike Harcourt as premier. And throughout all these changes there was the constancy of federal-provincial squabbling over jurisdictional responsibilities. "Many times, the Nisga'a ended up mediating between the federal and provincial governments," recalls Jim Aldridge, lead lawyer for the Nisga'a.

Although the Nisga'a were an extremely disciplined team and approached their job in a cordial and formal manner, negotiations were often intense and profoundly adversarial, and tempers did flare. On only one occasion did a Nisga'a negotiator insult a government official, remarkable given the intensity and long duration of the talks. In general Aldridge was the Nisga'a's designated "ranter," and he could and did blast away at the negotiators from both senior governments. "There were times when things got very heated," he says.

There were times when we would just bog down. The high degree of mutual respect that existed at the table in no way altered the fact that there were deep differences of opinion and difficult negotiations, and it took a long time to either persuade one party or the other to change their position. More likely, to creatively find a solution that met the needs of all sides. And then once that formulation had been agreed to at the table, both governments had to run it through their respective approval systems in Victoria and Ottawa. It was often a hideously slow process, but I would not attribute any part of the delay to a lack of effort or

Harry Nyce, Nisga'a negotiator and fisheries expert. *Gary Fiegehen photo* capability by the people who sat across the table. The negotiating teams could not be held responsible for any of the delays. These were the result of institutional problems, endemic to this country, a Canadian reluctance to try out new ideas. Of course, there were political and media fears as well.

Somewhat curiously, Aldridge absolves politicians for the glacial pace of the talks, other than to note their reluctance to make decisions. Instead, he places the blame on senior bureaucrats in Ottawa and Victoria, who dreamed up the reasons why one Nisga'a initiative after another could not be accommodated. However, at times the politicians did take the lead, slowing the pace as they became ambivalent, frightened or hostile after looking over the treaty briefing papers crossing their desks. For example, it was a politician,

DIAND Minister Jane Stewart, who appeared to decide for her own political reasons to table the introduction of the Nisga'a bill in Parliament in the spring of 2000, thus delaying it to the fall when a new minister, Robert Nault, took over.

There were also times when it appeared that the pace of the talks was slowed by the cautious and consensual style of Nisga'a decision making. Each person at the table would be given the documents that were being discussed at the time—fisheries or

Joseph Gosnell during one of the seemingly endless negotiating sessions. *Gary Fiegehen photo* forests or subsurface rights—then day after day, year after year, they would pore over these documents, written by and for lawyers who had little interest in translating them into plain language. It's the law, it was explained. It has to be this way. Although for all the Nisga'a these negotiating sessions were complex, tedious and exhausting, it was hardest for the hereditary chiefs among them who seldom said much in the formal negotiations, and more than a few insiders wondered how much of this legalized table talk was actually comprehensible.

Most issues were also carefully considered in internal sessions where all aspects of the issue at hand would be scoped out in minute detail. While this allowed the Nisga'a to be fully briefed and cognizant of all possible scenarios, it could also slow the process considerably. Indeed, this need for consensus, so particular to many First Nations, stands in stark contrast to contemporary white management practice and underscores the cultural chasm between the two cultures. Oral societies such as the Nisga'a appear to find it difficult to allow for individual decisions or varieties of opinion when maintenance of group solidarity is the overriding concern, as was the case during the endless rounds of talks. In many ways, they appeared to actually think differently than their non-aboriginal adversaries, tending to be more holistic, showing greater attention to context and less dependence on logic. Non-native negotiators appeared more analytic, avoiding contradiction, focussing on objects removed from their context and being more reliant on logic.

The one person who successfully bestrode both worlds was Aldridge—a.k.a. The Chess Master. As directed by the Nisga'a, he was both architect and protector of the treaty, an obsessed man labouring over its every clause and semicolon and a street fighter who never hesitated to take on his adversaries with a formidable left hook. An intellectual pugilist, he had little time for those he considered cerebrally challenged. The negotiating room was his fight ring, his place to shine, where after thousands of hours of intense wrangling he emerged bloody but unbowed with a defensible treaty for his client. Fiercely protective of the Nisga'a, he rode herd on the other white consultants, serving as the trusted middleman who could

explain and interpret the cultural subtleties of tribal council management, which to outsiders could sometimes appear confusing. Savage in his assessment of those who could not, or would not, parry at his level, he would dismiss some treaty critics as intellectual inferiors. He could and would articulate Nisga'a anger against white people. "Don't be so ethnocentric," he'd snap if a consultant were foolish enough to stumble into politically incorrect territory.

Aldridge appeared unwilling—or unable—to reduce complicated treaty realities into the simple messages that are the standard fare of the media and popular culture. Like all lawyers, he relies on the power and persuasion of words, using the English language in a narrow and specific manner, thinking in terms of legal authority, clarity and precision where there is no room for ambiguity. His emphasis is on

Jim Aldridge, lawyer for the Nisga'a, with his wife
Ellen at a celebration in Gitwinksihlkw, 2000.
Gary Fiegehen photo

legal precedent, negotiations and privileged communication. When Mark Hume, fisheries specialist and a senior reporter at the *Vancouver Sun*, asked for an explanation of the fisheries component of the treaty, Aldridge splashed numbers and charts all over the white board in a meeting room at his offices in the Marine Building. The reporter watched and listened intently. Interconnected and interrelated catch, run, harvest, escapement and allocation statistics came fast and furiously for more than an hour, at which time the reporter closed up his notebook and admitted he didn't clearly understand the difference between the treaty entitlement and the harvest agreement of the salmon stocks. Aldridge was crestfallen; the meeting was over. Seconds after Hume stepped into the elevator and the doors clicked into place, Aldridge had summarily dismissed him with a wave of his hand as if he was just another dimwit who didn't get it. The following day, Hume phoned a Nisga'a media consultant to advise, "Tell your client the fish stuff was far too complicated. I didn't get a word of it. Waste of time. Better make it understandable for the media and the public if you really want to be able to sell it."

Perhaps Aldridge's disappointment wasn't with the reporter but the realization that the biggest accomplishment of his life—the intricacies of BC's first modern treaty—may never be properly recognized or understood. Artists have the gratification of watching an audience respond to their work; authors get reviewed. But Aldridge had laboured for all those years yet couldn't be a hero because, while the general public might appreciate the idea of the treaty and what it represented, only a small circle of lawyers and insiders knew the genius that went into the deal.

During the later years of the negotiations, Aldridge, a self-described control freak and monomaniac, would play

"Minesweeper" on his laptop while the other parties deliberated their next move. At the end of the day when the team members, both white and aboriginal, gravitated to the hotel bar to recap the day's events and let off steam, he could hold forth—a non-stop talker, cigarette and beer in hand—until he retired to his hotel room to play the acoustic guitar he lugged along with him. A clever wit, his monologues—he brokered no competition unless it was from his Nisga'a client—resembled a kind of nightclub patter with quick turns and clever asides. Respected, admired, even loved by some of the Nisga'a elite, he was the intellectual force behind a treaty that would divide the country. But the years took their toll on Aldridge, too. When I drove him to his home on the west side of Vancouver one evening, he turned to me as he got out of the car, his complexion an unhealthy pallor. "I just want it to be over," he said, his hands shaking. "I want to do something else with my life. I'm a negotiator, not an administrator." But there seemed so much administrating to do. And once inside the room it was his job to focus the talks, and it seemed at times that it was only his skilful coercions that seemed to keep the team on track.

By the time the raucous debates over the Nisga'a Treaty were singeing the air in legislatures in Victoria and Ottawa, the face of the treaty as far as most Canadians were concerned was Joseph Gosnell, Sim'oogit Hleek, a hereditary chief of the Eagle Clan. His statesmanlike public presentation—moderate, credible, and trustworthy—was destined to win the day in the court of public opinion and effectively repel a series of wilting attacks from opposition politicians and critics. A shy yet stubborn man, he was catapulted into the spotlight by the death of his older brother James, the firebrand who had set the stage for modern Nisga'a treaty

Joseph and Adele Gosnell in the backyard of their
home in Gitlakdamiks. *Gary Fiegehen photo*

making. But while his brother's death cast a permanent shadow on Joseph's life, it also marked his ascendancy within
Nisga'a politics. In 1990 he was elected as the fourth president—Frank Calder, his brother James and Alvin McKay
had preceded him—of the Nisga'a Tribal Council, which had
supplanted the old Land Committee in 1955. As president
he became the lead negotiator during the formal treaty talks,
and as the debate over the Nisga'a Treaty intensified, he
emerged as its best and truest salesman. Revelling in his public role, comfortable in the media spotlight, he grew naturally into the job. "Joe was a brilliant presenter of the treaty,"
says Frank Calder, "able to simply and powerfully communi-
cate complicated concepts to the public and media."

Lawyer Jim Aldridge, who had worked with three presi-
dents—James Gosnell, Alvin McKay and Joseph Gosnell—
noted that despite profound differences in personality, style
and skill, there remained throughout an astonishing degree
of political continuity. "That continuity tells me that the
leadership of the Nisga'a is, and always has been, more than

Joseph Gosnell, Alvin McKay and Jim Aldridge
during a negotiating session. *Gary Fiegehen photo*

personality dominated." In his view that leadership for the
last twenty years has comprised "the entire set of individuals—chief counsellors, executive members and staff positions—that remained remarkably intact despite various
changes at the top. And the style that the leader has always
adopted has been that of a person who would embody and
epitomize the values and skills that were shared by the group
rather than everybody following behind a singular charismatic leader. It is not fair, therefore, to say that Gosnell was the
primary actor from the Nisga'a team; he was an important
player among many."

Among the many others to whom Aldridge was referring is
Edmond Wright, the sharpest mind on the Nisga'a team; in
fact, Aldridge was often heard to say that Wright was the only
one who knew the treaty as well as he did himself. Indeed, it
was Wright's comprehensive grasp of the *Indian Act*, mastery

Edmond Wright with former federal negotiator
David Osborne. *Gary Fiegehen photo*

of band bureaucracy and administration, grasp of financial affairs, and ability to make quick decisions that others could recognize and follow that made him a formidable adversary. And on more than one occasion his intimidating physical presence brought other members of the Nisga'a team into line.

Wright, whose Nisga'a name is Galgyookskw, seemed an anomaly among the members of the Nisga'a team. Born in Gitlakdamiks in 1945 into the Wolf clan, he was not high-born like Gosnell and had to work his way to the top. At age fourteen he was sent to a United Church residential school in Edmonton. For three years he served in the Army Reserves: ever the pragmatist, he was willing to trade his free-dom for tangible gain, in this case real cream in his coffee and real butter on his bread. "Army food was far better than the canned pork they fed us at the residential school," he recalled. Upon high school graduation, he left Edmonton and returned to the Nass River Valley. There he met and mar-ried Millicent Clayton; they raised two girls and a boy.

To earn a living, Wright worked in the canneries, on fish packers and in the Port Edward pulp mill as a heavy machine operator. He tried his hand at logging and at one point con-sidered a career in social work. But in 1970 he accepted a job as Gitlakdamiks band manager, taking quickly to the compli-cated formulas of federal and provincial funding, grants and systems. Over the years he became a skilled money man, las-soing money for the people of his village. In 1973 he ran for political office, winning election as a local trustee on the trib-al council; he has been a fixture there ever since. During treaty negotiations, Wright's colleagues relied on his ability to make sense of the complicated concepts built into the treaty but, perhaps more importantly, relied on him to explain its

essence to the Nisga'a people in language they could understand. As a result, Wright enjoys the genuine respect of the
Nisga'a people. Now fifty-five, he is considered by many of
them to be a symbol of the new meritocracy the Nisga'a government will have to develop in order to create a viable economy in the Nass River.

A decision maker, he makes things happen, though he can
sometimes appear gruff and intimidating. Once asked if he
was planning a summer vacation, he growled, "Indians making treaties don't take holidays." When explaining the treaty
to politicians or answering charges from critics, Wright
eschewed jargon to make his points. "Many commentators
have stated that we were going to become an autonomous
nation state," he told the provincial Select Standing
Committee on Aboriginal Affairs on September 17, 1996.
"Nothing could be further from the truth. We have clearly
indicated, especially through the opening remarks of our
president, that we are negotiating our way into Canada and
British Columbia. We have clearly stated that the Charter of
Rights and Freedoms will apply to the lands and to our people. We have also stated that the administration of justice
arrangements is fully integrated into the overall justice system of the province under the authority of the Attorney
General. I think it's also very important to note that there are
very few areas where our laws will prevail. They are mainly in
regard to our lands and our culture, those types of things.
But certainly federal and provincial laws of general application will apply." He concluded his presentation by putting a
financial spin on a standard Nisga'a theme: the desire to join
Canada as a free and equal people. "We want to live like anybody else in British Columbia, whereby your investment in a
home becomes worth something in the future. Today we

don't have that. We can build pretty nice homes in our communities today, but there is no market value for them because it's restricted to Indian people to access that property. We would certainly be making those kinds of laws."

His years of dedication to treaty making have not quelled Wright's impish and infectious sense of humour, and a comment from him could change the tone of the most tense negotiating session. I am particularly reminded of an occasion in the mid-1990s when I had become concerned about the increasing column inches of anti-treaty commentary in the print media. I requested a session with the tribal council bosses to impress upon them the need to develop a new media strategy to stem the rising tide of bad press, and they summoned me to Terrace for an hour's appearance at a meeting. As a behind-the-scenes wordsmith, I am uncomfortable about making public presentations, even to a client I had worked with for so long, and I became convinced I would need a novel talking point or visual cue to make my point to Wright, Gosnell and company. Walking down Lakelse Avenue on my way to the Terrace Inn for the meeting, I noticed the All Seasons Source for Sports store, with all the latest golf, hunting and basketball equipment gleaming in its front window. With no real sense of purpose, I wandered in and studied the inventory. Then, spotting the bins of softballs and hardballs, I asked the owner if I could borrow one of each for an hour or two. He said yes and I headed down the street to meet the Nisga'a crew.

It was a bad day for a spin doctor. Everyone in the room looked beat and bored. The day's agenda, long and daunting, was already well behind schedule. Eventually the chair of the meeting announced me to the room and I stood in showman fashion to make my pitch. "I've got two balls," I said in my most stentorian baritone. "Now is the time for the tribal council to stop playing softball (one ball was held up) and start playing hardball (the other ball)." There was silence. And more silence as I placed the two balls on the table in front of me so that I could fish a longish memo out of my pocket. Suddenly Wright barked out: "So do the Nisga'a. We Nisga'a already have two balls!" All the chiefs and politicians began to hoot with laughter, many repeating the phrase again and again. I tried to sputter on, but the joke was on me. Against all this hilarity, it was difficult to get my carefully planned presentation over to the meeting. I returned the balls to the store and caught the evening plane back to Vancouver. But next morning, I received a fax authorizing the green light for the hardball strategy.

Nelson Leeson was the Nisga'a negotiator who reminded me most of the mischievous Raven of Nisga'a myth. A gifted raconteur with the timing of a nightclub comedian, he is a genuinely funny man, who could and would entertain until closing time when we all gathered in the bar after a long day. He was popular with many white consultants, speaking their language, teasing, thanking them, making them feel part of the team. But it was his oratory and ability to summarize complicated concepts that made him valuable at the negotiating table.

In his youth he had been a graceful natural athlete, one of the finest basketball players—white or aboriginal—to come out of the North Coast. Often on the same teams as his close friend, Edmond Wright, he would shoot out the lights with his jump shot, while Wright, the short, high-energy point guard, set up the plays. High-born, groomed for great things by his family and village, Leeson dissipated part of his youth in bars and bar fights, becoming a scrapper of considerable

reputation. In more recent years, although he no longer drinks, his lifestyle returned to haunt him; he suffers from serious diabetes, a disease that has been devastating to so many aboriginal people.

During my first assignment to Nisga'a territory in 1989, Leeson proved a generous and witty host, proudly introducing me to some of the people and places of his Nass homeland.

Nisga'a negotiator Nelson Leeson on the docks at Lakalzap. *Gary Fiegehen photo*

After we attended a feast at Gitwinksihlkw, which lasted well past midnight—an exhausting experience for a visitor—he offered to put me up for the night, an offer I quickly accepted. Driving home slowly through the lava fields, navigating the switchbacks of the central Nass Valley, through the spruce forest and all the way to the bridge that crosses the Nass River near his home village of Lakalzap, he fielded my endless and naive questions about Nisga'a culture and customs. In the middle of the concrete span, he shut off the motor of his truck and let the vehicle roll to a stop. He climbed out of the cab and walked down the bridge and into the night. It was silent except for the churning of the river below. Jagged stars flared across the northern sky. Suddenly he reappeared in the headlights to fling his long arms wide into the night. "We are all human beings," he shouted. "We all need a place to live. The Nass is our place."

But Leeson's very humanness made him all the more vulnerable as he dealt with the glacial pace and seemingly endless years of negotiations. And how those years changed him, taking a terrible toll on such a mercurial psyche in the prime of his life. But duty-bound, like all his colleagues, he soldiered on.

With the possible exception of Joseph Gosnell, Rod Robinson, with his handsome mane of silver hair testifying to the fifty years he has worked to settle the land question, is the most photographed of all the Nisga'a leaders. A hereditary chief of the Eagle clan—his Nisga'a name is Mineesq—for many people he personifies the implacable patience and tenacity that led the team to success. Asked how he felt on May 13, 2000, when the treaty was ratified on Parliament Hill, he said simply, "Free. I felt free. As a person who lived most of his life under the *Indian Act*, I felt like a free man."

Now sixty-nine years old, Robinson's life has been defined by personal struggle. Born in Gitlakdamiks he, like others of his generation, was sent away at the age of eight to St. Michael's Residential School near Alert Bay. At seventeen he attended high school in Prince Rupert, a city that was closer to home and friendlier as many other Nisga'a lived and worked there in the canneries and at other labouring jobs. After school, he unloaded fish at Sunnyside Cannery—a dirty job, he recalls—then graded fish at a cold storage plant. In those days traditional Nisga'a culture was derided by non-aboriginals as a nuisance that interfered with commerce. "They sneered at us," he says.

Staying to work "on the outside" Robinson became a fish-grader foreman, but after five years bought a gillnetter and later worked on a seine boat. But as fishing was—and still is—a seasonal occupation, he went ashore for good when he saw a poster advertising jobs for loggers. He made big money in the woods, working his way up from chokerman to faller, from boom foreman to river-drive foreman, from cat and skidder driver to loader operator and again to foreman. In 1952 he married Marjorie Clayton and together they raised ten children, seven boys and three girls.

In 1985 he was hired by the tribal council and took his place with the representatives of the

Rod Robinson at Old Aiyansh. *Gary Fiegehen photo*

four clans in the deliberations to develop strategies to settle the land question. "Yes, I grew old in the struggle for justice. But all the sacrifices, all the heartaches were worth it," he says. "But sometimes it hurt being away from home, especially during winter when conditions in the Nass can be harsh. We worried so much about our families." Robinson confidently predicts that over time the treaty will change attitudes as a new generation of Nisga'a and their non-aboriginal neighbours work and live side by side in the Pacific Northwest Corridor. He appears to bear no malice toward those who opposed the deal. "Our ancient code instructs us not to use strong language, not to insult those who oppose us. We are taught to respect everyone's way of life," says Robinson, but he adds, "Share our land, yes. But never give it away."

The Nisga'a team set out the parameters for a deal that, once ratified, would be the first in Canada—the first in the world—to include self-government as an integral component of the land claims agreement. Further complexity and controversy was added because the treaty was also the first in Canadian history to deal with a major commercial resource: the salmon fisheries of the Nass River. In the end, the negotiations resulted in a treaty and a triumph for the Nisga'a team, but seen another way, those twenty-three years of negotiations added up to a failure of government policy and a repudiation of federal and provincial efforts, no matter how honourable and well-intended, to settle the "Indian Question." The process amounted to a colossal waste of human potential—a Canadian tragedy that took a devastating human toll on Chief Gosnell and his colleagues, whose faces and body language, beyond any words, tell a story of unutterable loneliness and weariness.

CHAPTER SEVEN

The Dreams of a Fisherman

A basic fact in the world of communications consulting is that today's media must put a face to an issue, and when I was hired as a consultant for the Nisga'a Tribal Council, it was understood that part of my job was to develop strategies to raise Joseph Gosnell's profile. As far as my job was concerned, his greatest natural gift was an ability to stay above the fray, to remain dignified and statesmanlike during the ugliest and most rancorous episodes of the debate. Standing firmly on higher ground, appealing to the better nature of the Canadian public that had grown to trust and empathize with him, he was

Eulachon fishing in Fishery Bay.
Gary Fiegehen photo

able to convey the public impression that he was able to resist the insidious ideological gamesmanship without the coarsening of mind that comes from doing battle.

Straddling two cultures, Gosnell masterfully played a role that would bring the treaty home to his people. As part of the Nisga'a negotiations team, he dutifully attended internal caucus sessions in which every strategy, every compromise was talked out, every team member expressing his view, collectively agonizing over decisions that would affect their people forever. Often, while they deliberated, Gosnell would be interrupted by a phone call from a reporter and leave the room to answer it. He was part of the team, yes; indeed, he held the titular title of lead negotiator. But like many leaders he projected an authoritarian solitude and kept a careful distance from his colleagues. Most of the team stayed at the

Joseph Gosnell, respected and often quoted by the media, grants another interview. By the time the treaty was introduced into the House of Commons, he had become the most high-profile aboriginal leader in the country. *Gary Fiegehen photo*

Chateau Granville Hotel; Gosnell would take a room at another hotel, a few blocks away. But his public persona hardly revealed the whole man. A man whose early adult life was defined by a debilitating sense of shyness, a tall man standing in the shadows—watching, always watching—as charismatic brother James took centre stage. In a classic case of sibling drama, it was only his brother's tragic death that set the stage for Joseph's ascension in Nisga'a politics and later, to the national stage. Only then did the awkward man with the big shoulders and big smile, whose view of the world was learned at the helm of his father's gillnetter, begin his metamorphosis: slowly and uncertainly at first, but quickly learning his new role, he emerged as the most respected First Nations leader of the present day, both in Canada and around the world.

Joseph Gosnell was born at the small Arrandale cannery near Gingolx at the mouth of the Nass River on June 21, 1936, one of the twelve children—six boys and six girls— of Mary Moore and Eli Gosnell, a hereditary chief of the Eagle clan. Eli was a deeply religious man who became an envoy in the Salvation Army and insisted on a strict upbringing for his children, both in the Christian faith and in the traditional culture of his people. "He never

Joseph Gosnell in front of Victoria's Legislative Buildings, where, on December 2, 1998, he delivered one of the most dramatic speeches in modern Canadian history.

allowed us to do anything on Sunday, even when we were teenagers," Gosnell recalls. "And both my mother and my father made sure we adhered to the Nisga'a customs and traditions." Other relatives also instilled lessons in tribal culture:

> In the fall of 1942, Uncle Harry shot a grizzly and brought it back home in his canoe. I was about seven years old at the time. He called me down to the bank of the river where the grizzly had been pulled ashore—myself, my brother Benny and my cousin Arthur Moore. My uncle then pulled apart its giant mouth and told each of us to put our faces right inside the huge jaw and teeth. He said to each of us: "When you grow up you will be like this bear. You will fear no one, you will not back away, you will defend and guard what is yours—with your life."

But by this time much had already been taken away or destroyed. Playing in the crawl space under his grandfather's house in Gitwinksihlkw, the young Joseph Gosnell did not understand why anyone would carve such beautiful figures on the dusty wooden beams. It was only years later, after returning from residential school, that he realized the foundations of his grandfather's house had once been the towering Nisga'a totem poles that graced the main street of the remote village. "Before they were allowed to embrace Christianity, they had to deny their own spiritual beliefs. Other totem poles were chopped down and floated down river where they were 'boomed up' and milled in Prince Rupert." He played in the long grass beside the Nass, and in their own small canoes he and his friends paddled the river's complicated tides and whirling currents. In those days, long before the road was built from Terrace, the river was the highway to the Nisga'a villages, serving both as an obstacle to prosperity and a geographical line of defence against further incursions by white settler society.

In 1943, when he was seven years old, the government intervened in Gosnell's life in dramatic fashion: the local Indian Agent decreed that all Nisga'a children were to be sent away to a church-run residential school. He was one of fifteen Nisga'a children lined up to board a steamship idling at the wharf of the Inverness Cannery near Prince Rupert. His mother stood by, weeping. "As I stood on the dock with my brother Ben, my mother kept saying to us in Nisga'a—we didn't know any English then—'You are going away to learn, to learn and to be educated.'"

After a two-day sea voyage, with stops at Klemtu and River's Inlet to pick up more aboriginal children, the steamship arrived at St. Michael's Residential School (Anglican), a foreboding structure in Alert Bay on Cormorant Island north of Campbell River. For the next six

St. Michael's Residential School near Alert Bay on Vancouver Island where Joseph Gosnell was sent as a young boy. *BC Archives H-02890*

years, Gosnell would learn to survive a very harsh discipline. Although he neither experienced nor even heard rumours of the sexual abuse and physical brutality that occurred in other residential schools, St. Michael's was not an easy experience. "That was a rough life. The discipline was extremely hard. Oh, well do I know the taste of soap!" he says, recalling the Anglican brothers washing his mouth out with soap for speaking Nisga'a. "Every night you could hear children crying in the dormitories." Forbidden to speak their own language, the Nisga'a children would whisper secretly to each other in Nisga'a, but over time English became the common language. Like many aboriginal people of his generation, Gosnell recalls always being hungry. "We never had enough to eat and we had to eat the food that was placed before us, whether we liked it or not."

Despite the suppression of his language and culture in the prison-like buildings so far from home, always running through his dreams was the great, dark Nass from which his people draw their very identity—the first schools of eulachon in spring and the silver flash of the first coho salmon as they enter the river. "I've been to the headwaters of the Nass," he will say today. "At Meziadin Lake the water is so clear you can see four hundred feet down into the lake."

Today, the sixty-four-year-old Gosnell does not blame his parents for sending him away. "Like all Nisga'a parents they faced incredible psychological intimidation to conform. They were ordered by the Indian Agent to send us away, part of the assimilation policy. On the contrary, I thank them for what they did for me, instilled in me the importance of the culture that we maintain today. My mother always said, 'Don't ever forget our language.'" He has never considered suing the church or the federal government for his treatment

Joseph Gosnell stoops to drink from the icy and
pristine waters of Nass Lake. *Gary Fiegehen photo*

at St. Michael's, but he says, "I wouldn't want to put my children through the same thing—never in a thousand years."

> When I first arrived at St. Michael's, I didn't know a word of English, not even a "yes" or a "no." When I came out of there after six years, I had almost forgotten my own language. We were little kids; we didn't even know we were Indians then. We watched so many cowboy and Indian movies, and we always rooted for the guys with the ten-gallon hats. It explains to some extent the dysfunctional nature of some of our people. When you are taken away from your parents at a young stage, removed from a closely knit family and placed in a completely alien atmosphere, you lose an important sense of parental guidance. I see that happening today and it is like a sickness passed from one generation to the next. Very few people recognize that. It explains the depression you see in the faces of the people, the alcoholism, and now the drugs.

At St. Michael's, Gosnell learned to read and write the English language and counted among his classmates a generation of men who would one day become leaders in the struggle for aboriginal rights. The friendships he forged then against the common enemy would later translate into political support. "Whenever the tribal groups from across the province meet, I greet my friends from those days," Gosnell says. "It taught me discipline. It put backbone in my spine. I walked away from that and I knew I could stand up to anything." He also met his future wife, Adele, there—she had arrived from the Nass on a later steamship—though mostly he only watched her across the strictly segregated play-ground. They married in 1957 and raised six of their own children and one whom they adopted. In May 1999 Gosnell and his wife returned to visit St. Michael's for a reunion to mark the centenary of its construction. "We met one friend we hadn't seen since Grade One."

The Gosnells were a fishing family. Father Eli was a boat-builder, producing twenty-five gillnet boats prized by the North Coast salmon fleet. Joseph's mother and aunts would gut and clean the salmon when the men returned from the sea. Some of his earliest memories stem from his days on the deck of his father's gillnetter, with big brother James also on board as the three navigated the choppy waters of Observatory Inlet or, farther to the west, the dangerous pas-sageways of Hecate Strait. Like his father, like all fishermen, Joseph would later learn to hold two thoughts in particular at bay: fears about his family—because only in very serious cases involving his immediate family would he get a call on the VHF radio—and regret over things he had said or done in the past. His years at sea conditioned him to the dispro-portion of sea and land, to differing perspectives of time and space.

It is not surprising that one of Gosnell's defining experi-ences would take place on these icy waters. It happened on September 28, 1972. While most Canadians were watching Paul Henderson bang the puck past Vladislav Tretiak to win game eight of the first Canada-Russia hockey series, Gosnell was simply trying to stay alive on the storm-tossed waters of the Hecate Strait as he headed home from the south end of the Queen Charlottes. He was alone aboard the *Miss Marilyn*, named for his first daughter. James, then president of the Nisga'a Tribal Council, was skippering his own boat,

PE 259. Eli was piloting the *Lady G.* The wind had been picking up steadily out of the southeast all afternoon. "We knew there was a storm coming," Joseph says in recollection. "We made our decision to try and beat it back [to the mainland] from the Queen Charlottes. Big mistake. It caught us halfway home."

What had begun as fitful gusts was soon blowing at more than 100 knots, lashing the crests of the icy swells into lacy

Joseph Gosnell in front of his eleven-metre gillnetter, the *Nishga'a Cloud*, moored at Port Edward.
Gary Fiegehen photo

white spray that drummed against the cabin glass. The deck tilted as the *Miss Marilyn* plunged in the sea, heading northeast to Prince Rupert. As the fury of the North Pacific came up on the quarter beam, the boat was rolling so much that he couldn't take his hands off the wheel. The deck then tipped into an almost vertical position as waves smashed over the boat and the stern filled up with water. Now the vessel was wallowing, making it almost impossible to steer. At the bottom of each trough Gosnell was looking straight up into a wall of water ahead and a steep hill of water surging up behind.

He had already climbed into his survival suit, the insulated flotation device that might give him a few more hours of life in the frigid waters. "Twice I almost walked off the boat," he says. "The waves were coming right over her. I took all my personal ID and I taped it to my chest so that when they found my remains, they'd know who I was." Eventually the trio of boats limped past the lighthouse at Vanilla Island to safe anchorage at Banks Island, surviving a storm none would ever forget. "What should have been a ten-hour trip took eighteen hours," Gosnell remembers.

In the years following his brother's death, Joseph began to take a more active interest in the political life of his people, first in village, then in band politics. After first paying his dues in a number of supporting political roles, in 1990 he was elected president of the Tribal Council, winning re-election three times. The examples set by his father, Eli, and brother James have been crucial to the development of his own leadership skills and the soft-spoken but tough-minded diplomacy that would come to characterize his political style. James's influence has been the most profound. "He and I fished many, many years together. In the confined space of a fishing boat, you get to know your partner very, very well. You know everything your older brother says and does." But he would need, as well, all of the self-reliance he had learned at the wheel of his own gillnetter to ride out the fierce storms of political protest. And when it came time to take on his treaty critics, he emerged as a lethally effective practitioner of high-stakes political debate, which is not, of course, like other forms of debate. It is not primarily a dispassionate, logical argument in which ideas are pitted against each other to see which is most compelling. It is debate as combat, in which the contest of ideas is subordinate to the struggle for dominance between the debaters. Victory requires knowing all the weaknesses of the opposition, and after a life of speech making it's no surprise that Gosnell should excel at that. But it also requires a taste for face-to-face confrontation and a sense of high style and showmanship. Here, too, once he rehearsed his lines and worked with his advisors to control his temper, Gosnell predictably excelled. As a result the media and the general public perceived him as the face of the treaty. If there was very little lightness, modesty or self-awareness in the high-road persona Gosnell and his advisers crafted, his public presentation was consistently statesman-like and regal. And if at times this seemingly unknowable man displayed an exaggerated sense of his own entitlement and a monumental egotism, both are best viewed through the perspective of a traditional Nisga'a culture, where chiefs are expected to regally represent their people as a whole.

But he took his knocks, as well. By the time the Agreement in Principle (pre-cursor to the final treaty) was initialled on August 4, 1998, in Gitlakdamiks, he had become a significant national figure, whose image often flickered on the nightly news. And as the Gosnell star began to shine brightly, grumbling from the supporting cast could be heard offstage. *Sotto voce* at first, this sniping grew louder as Gosnell received honourary degrees from universities, the Order of British Columbia and other prestigious humanitarian awards. His vulnerabilities were savoured by his detractors, though to his admirers, they made him seem more human than some of his contemporaries. In difficult tense situations, Gosnell would begin to hum loudly, perhaps a kind of whistling in the dark, unconscious compensation for a frightened little boy trapped in the gloom of residential school.

Joseph Gosnell receiving a humanitarian award
from Bob White of the Canadian Labour Congress.
Gary Fiegehen photo

And year after year, during open-mike sessions at Nisga'a annual conventions, former Gingolx resident Mercy Thomas (now living in the town of Cloverdale) would decry what she described as the elitism and all-male cronyism of Gosnell and the Nisga'a leaders, complaining they had little contact with people in the Nass villages. Originally a supporter of the treaty process, she had turned dramatically against the deal and the negotiating team when it was announced that much of Gingolx traditional territory was not protected as "core land" within the treaty. Since that day she has attacked the deal with the ferocity of the betrayed. And while she was indisputably right in saying that the negotiations schedules had turned Gosnell and his colleagues into absent and part-time fathers and residents, it is unfair to claim this was a lifestyle he would willingly have chosen for himself. In fact, during the long years of negotiations, conversations with Gosnell would return again and again to a common motif: his thoughts of his family and his friends and neighbours in his Nass River home.

However, Thomas was right about the absence of women from the negotiations. In fact, many observers were struck by the mostly male dynamics of all three negotiating teams where, with the exception of several female lawyers, women worked only in supporting or secretarial roles. The Nisga'a team included only two women, both of them acting as secretaries. All the leaders were male, and like all men in groups there seemed to be such a close and unhealthy intensity of

After receiving an honourary degree at Royal Roads University in Victoria, Joseph Gosnell addresses the graduating class. *Gary Fiegehen photo* pant-hitching, male posturing and testosterone poisoning that visitors scrambled to open a window. On several occasions, white communications consultants raised this issue to the tribal council brass, diplomatically pointing out that, in the court of public opinion, it was important for Nisga'a women to be seen walking in concert with Chief Gosnell and others, especially when the red lights of the television cameras were turned on. On each occasion, these public relations proposals were carefully considered, then politely rejected. And when reporters asked Chief Gosnell about the absence of Nisga'a women on his team, there followed a careful explication to the effect that Nisga'a society was a matrilineal one in which women exercised their power behind the throne by influencing and imparting important knowledge.

Over time, and sometimes to the dismay of his colleagues and handlers, it became increasingly evident that Joseph Gosnell was following no one's script but his own. Stubborn, willful on occasion, or filled with a righteous anger, he possessed a singular drive to bring a modern treaty home to his people. However, he was always a courteous and active listener who respected the opinions of others—unless they presented an obstruction to the aspirations of his people or were guilty of human rights abuses.

This was demonstrated in Vancouver on Sunday night, November 12, 1997, when a crush of protesters, pressing against the barricades and a wall of police, taunted more than eight hundred guests entering the Hyatt Regency Hotel for a $1,000-a-plate dinner, a public relations initiative by the city for the Asian Pacific Economic Conference (APEC) week. Nothing had been left to chance. Everyone had been briefed. Inside the hotel the guest of honour, Chinese

President Jiang Zemin, took his seat and prepared for the rit-
ual offering of salmon, speeches and photo opportunities for
a phalanx of international media. Everything went according
to plan—that is, until Gosnell stepped to the microphone.

Gosnell and other members of the tribal council had
received formal invitations to attend this APEC dinner, and
he was to appear on the dais with heads of state to offer a
prayer honouring Jiang Zemin, the leader of one-quarter of
the world's population. They had accepted at the urging of
Adele Hurley, a Toronto-based lobbyist hired by the Nisga'a
to shepherd the treaty through its "eastern campaign" and
the debate on Parliament Hill. In an earlier incarnation,
Hurley had been instrumental in getting acid rain legislation
passed in both Canada and the US. She was comfortable in
the corridors of power and, with her network of contacts, was
able to affect such invitations because she was raised in tony
Oakville and counted among her clients and contacts some
of eastern Canada's media and intellectual elite. Attractive
and elegantly dressed, she was also to prove a curiosity to the
all-male platoon of Nisga'a negotiators. Late one October
afternoon as the APEC summit approached, Gosnell and his
team huddled around a table at the Chateau Granville Hotel
as Hurley laid out the tactics for their presence at the dinner.
This was good news, she explained. The event would provide
an ideal opportunity to raise the profile of the treaty by
reminding influential decision makers—public and private—
that a global audience was witness to the way Canada treated its aboriginal peoples.

As history would later confirm, Gosnell was the only one
on the dais that night who acknowledged and connected the
APEC summit with the clamour for human rights going on
outside. Everyone else pretended that they did not exist. "I

ask you to remember," he said in his prayer, "those people whose views I believe must be taken into consideration." It was only a single sentence, but he left no doubt in anyone's mind that he was referring to the protesters outside, brandishing pictures of Jiang labelled "Keynote Despot" and demanding Tibetan and Taiwanese independence. He had the courage to speak his mind, linking the plight of aboriginal people in Canada with human rights abuses around the world. His remarks contrasted with those of Power Corp. president Andre Desmarais, who praised President Jiang's "enlightened leadership" of China, referring to him as the "scholarly statesman" who had met regularly with intellectuals during his tenure as mayor of Shanghai.

Gosnell had, of course, broken the rules of an unspoken contract. Irritating foreign affairs officials, he had refused to play the insider's game and stand at the podium as the token Indian. He also risked offending his own prime minister, whose support for the treaty would be sorely needed later in the House of Commons. It was a daring display of the intellectual honesty and courage that had advanced his people so many times in the past, and in the months to come, as debate on the treaty intensified, Gosnell, by now the heart and soul of the campaign, would need all his skills as a statesman in order to ratify an agreement that had become the crux of his intellectual life.

In November 1998, after being buoyed by a meeting with Prime Minister Chrétien in Ottawa, Gosnell departed for an eight-day speaking tour of Europe. He was accompanied by Peter Baird, a DIAND communications consultant and me. Designed to capitalize on keen European interest as well as to set up the upcoming debate in the BC Legislature, the trip was financed by the federal government and Hongkong Bank

of British Columbia (HSBC) executive Milton K. Wong who pressed a $5,000-cheque into my hand to pay for travel and accommodation. "I want Chief Gosnell to be treated with the respect he deserves," Wong said.

After an overnight flight from Montreal to Frankfurt and a two-hour train ride to Bonn, Germany, we were met by Walter Larink, Academic Relations Officer for the Canadian Embassy. Larink then whisked us to the nearby University of Bonn where Gosnell was introduced to embassy officials and to Lothear Honnighausen, head of the North American program at the university. After a brief reception, Gosnell addressed a large crowd of graduate students, faculty and embassy officials, telling them the treaty was "a triumph for the Nisga'a people." Next morning, embassy officials arranged a tour of the German Parliament, the Bundestag,

Joseph Gosnell and Vancouver bank executive Milton K. Wong. A committed advocate of multiculturalism, Wong used his considerable influence to foster support for the treaty. *Gary Fiegehen photo*

before we headed back to the train station, then on to
Frankfurt airport for a late night flight to Vienna where, over
the next two days, Gosnell would deliver a series of speeches
and seminars, patiently answering questions from students.
The keen level of interest shown by the European public and
media confirmed that the Nisga'a Treaty had become international news to many Europeans fascinated by North
American aboriginal art and culture.

As a first-time visitor to Europe, Gosnell was fascinated as
well. In the Netherlands, Austria and later in London, he
appeared overwhelmed by the crowds on the narrow cobbled
streets and in the cafes and train stations. Halfway through
the whirlwind tour, he appeared homesick and retired to his
hotel room after the day's events to rest and phone his wife
and family. The railway line from Bonn to Frankfurt paral-
leled the Rhine River, and Gosnell settled in to stare out the
window at the shifting riverscape with its barges and tour
boats backdropped by carefully manicured vineyards and
Gothic castles. "I *knew* something was missing here," he said
with a chuckle, pointing out the window. "They've cut all the
trees down. There are no forests left in Germany."

In Vienna the Gosnell entourage stayed in a one-star hotel
in the Jewish district of the old city, and the second night
there we were awakened by the sound of smashing bottles
and the loud, frightening voices of Austrian skinheads. Next
morning, climbing the stone steps near the main entrance of
the hotel, I learned the reason for the chilling night noise: at
the top of the steps was a small synagogue where, from the
shadows, emerged two Austrian soldiers with semi-automatic
weapons slung over their shoulders. They explained they
were assigned to protect the synagogue, and that during the
night, a group of thugs and skinheads had driven in from the

Austrian countryside to throw beer bottles and scream obscenities in their "celebration" of the sixtieth anniversary of Kristallnacht or Night of Broken Glass, the notorious night of Nazi violence against Jewish people in Germany on November 9, 1938. The toll from that one night of violence included ninety-one Jews killed, hundreds seriously injured, and thousands more humiliated and terrorized. About 7,500 Jewish businesses were gutted and an estimated 177 synagogues were burned or otherwise demolished as police watched.

And while Austrian students and their professors sat enthralled as Gosnell explained how the treaty would protect his peoples' rights and traditional culture, they were also grappling with an upswell of intolerance from within their own society. "Yuppie fascist" Jorg Haider's Freedom Party was emerging as Austria's second-largest party, raising widespread fears that Austria was ready to embrace a refurbished right-wing extremism carrying many of the hallmarks of the old Nazi rhetoric. Attacking the Austrian bureaucracy, Haider's anti-establishment populism, his championship of xenophobia, and his clever exploitation of narrowly based nationalist instincts were also serving to renew the old question marks about Austria's latent anti-Semitism and its unwillingness to recognize the truth of its Nazi past.

Despite the frenetic schedule—twelve venues in eight days—Gosnell revelled in his celebrity. In London, he was a late night guest on a BBC-4 radio show that was beamed around the world. At Cambridge University he took the time to clip and save the newspaper accounts of his visits. The tour was therapeutic for Gosnell, a respite from the endless negotiations back home. After the day's events, over a glass of wine and a plate of veal, he would grow reflective and share

aspects of his personality, which he carefully compartmental-
ized during negotiations. In the medieval university town of
Leiden in South Holland, he surprised Baird and me by
describing the numbing intergenerational effects of the residential school system that took aboriginal children away
from their parents. "We didn't get a chance to learn how to
be parents. We were children having children and that has
taken a devastating toll."

He also described the sexual abuse he witnessed in the
Nass. Describing sexual abuse as "a cancer that never dies,"
he told us of a Salvation Army minister working in the tiny,
isolated community of Gitwinksihlkw during the 1960s.
Salvation Army Captain William Gareth Douglas would
brazenly call young boys out of class for "medical exams" and
"fishing trips," then corner them in the school basement or in
his private quarters. When the children complained to their
parents and elders about the abuse, they were dismissed or
punished since Captain Douglas was, after all, a prominent
and praiseworthy figure of village life. A devious sociopath
who ingratiated himself to the Nisga'a community, Douglas
wasn't punished until his victims launched a 1996 civil suit
against the Salvation Army and the federal government that
had established the school. He was convicted in 1998 on
twelve criminal charges of sexual assault and was sentenced
to seven years in prison. Financial details of a settlement
have been kept confidential by agreement with the Salvation
Army and the federal government. North Vancouver psychi-
atrist Dr. Charles Brasfield later set up a program to help the
victims and their families deal with post-traumatic stress dis-
orders, depression, marital problems and substance abuse.
He reports that, while many of the men have responded well
to therapy, some still find it difficult to build and maintain

trusting relationships. Others continue to abuse drugs and alcohol, while a few still smoulder with rage.

At the final speech held at the Canadian Embassy in London, Gosnell spoke with distinction and grace of the Nisga'a struggle. The keen interest of all his European audiences and the positive reception he received boosted his confidence and confirmed the treaty was international news. On the plane back to Canada, we held a strategy session. In his speech to kick off debate over the treaty in the BC Legislature, now just two weeks away, he wanted to exploit the stark contrast between his experience in Europe and the parochial tone of the debate back home.

By January 1999, however, attacks by politicians and the media had become so strident that I asked the *Vancouver Sun* op-ed page editor if they would accept an article by Gosnell addressing the criticisms. That article, which ran in the January 29 issue as a *"Vancouver Sun* Forum," pointed out that the treaty was not a result of a recent initiative; the Nisga'a had been seeking it since early in the nineteenth century. It also explained that it was not, as the critics were saying, a "Glen Clark" deal, but a tripartite deal that had begun with negotiations with the federal government back in 1976, and that it was not intended as a "template" for all future treaties. It also responded to the critics who said that the Nisga'a Lands would be become an enclave to ghettoize the Nisga'a people and discussed the proposed land tenure and justice systems. It certainly did not quiet the critics but it provided accurate information for the general public.

CHAPTER EIGHT

The Opposition

B y the time Bill C-9 (the Nisga'a Treaty) was introduced for debate on Parliament Hill on October 19,
1999, its contents had already been the subject of
the longest legislative debate in British Columbia
history, exhausting 116 hours of MLAs' time over 29 days.
BC's Bill 51 (the Nisga'a Final Agreement Act) is huge in
nature and sweeping in effect, encompassing nearly 70 claus-
es of legislation, 206 pages of treaty and 468 pages of appen-
dices. When the government cut off debate on April 22,
1999, BC Liberal leader Gordon Campbell and his fellow
opposition MLAs had canvassed only 11 of the 22 chapters
in the treaty. Although they had covered forestry and fishery
issues as well as land questions and the proposed Nisga'a government structure, they claimed they would need another six

River view just below Nass Canyon.
Gary Fiegehen photo

weeks to finish their questions, having never touched on justice administration, taxation and dispute resolution methods. Aboriginal Affairs Minister Gordon Wilson admitted justice and taxation issues hadn't made it to the detailed debate stage, but he said they had been generally discussed in the months after the bill was introduced on November 30, 1998.

The Liberals complained they had not been given enough time to study the treaty. "This is the largest single piece of legislation we have ever had before us in the province of British Columbia," Campbell said on the day debate was cut off. "This is the first treaty that has been brought forward. Mr. Clark says it is going to be a template for future treaties. Surely we should know exactly what is taking place before this is imposed and pushed on the people of British Columbia." While the Liberals had clear political goals in questioning and criticizing the treaty, they defended their attacks by saying that they were elected to do a job, and that job meant holding the government's feet to the fire. They also claimed it was important to get the government's detailed answers recorded in Hansard, the official record of the legislature. Since that record is often used by the courts to help interpret the intent of government legislation, this statement led to speculation that Campbell and his party might have been bolstering a future legal case against the Nisga'a by attacking within the legislature.

While Campbell's Liberals subsequently voted against the treaty, it was not the treaty as a whole they objected to, only

BC Liberal Opposition Leader Gordon Campbell, who led the political charge against the treaty in BC.

key elements of it. Primarily, they called it's self-government provisions an illegal amendment to Canada's Constitution. They also spent a significant amount of time attempting to expose undisclosed costs and special deals in the treaty, and because of their efforts the government was forced to admit that it would be spending $30 million to build a road from Lakalzap to the isolated village of Gingolx at the mouth of the Nass—something not mentioned in the treaty—on top of the $41 million upgrade of the Nisga'a Highway, which was included. This road link to Gingolx had been a long-held dream of the Nisga'a. Even more controversial was the BC government's pro-Nisga'a advertising budget which increased from an intitial $2.3 million to more than $7 million. This amount did not include the salaries of the high-level communication officials responsible for carrying out the advertising campaign as they had been seconded from government ministries.

The fierce tone of the debate inside the House was further polarized by the political about-face of Premier Clark, who had candidly admitted during his first years as a cabinet minister that he had no interest in or specific knowledge of aboriginal issues. But by the fall of 1998, he had become the Nisga'a Treaty's strongest supporter, calling it a basic human rights issue and criticizing naysayers as racists. An aggressive and partisan politician, he was clearly the driving force behind making the Nisga'a Treaty a provincial political issue, and insiders speculated that the NDP had set out to achieve a significant increase in public opinion polls by promoting the treaty. Hopefully it would rally the social democratic wing of the NDP and unbalance the Liberal opposition by pitting the right and left wings against one another, thus dividing provincial voters and allowing him to win another term. But with his

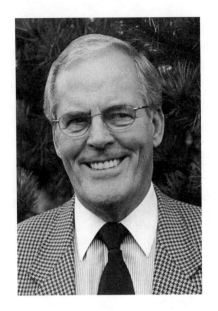

personal credibility badly damaged by a series of political crises, British Columbians were reticent to endorse anything Glen Clark was aggressively supporting, and public opinion polls at this time showed a drop in support for the deal in this province. And while it did unite the NDP, it never split the Liberal opposition.

The Liberals, however, were not the only ones to express concern over the government's use of closure. Nisga'a elder Frank Calder, who often watched events from the public gallery, expressed disappointment that debate was prematurely terminated, although he irritated other Nisga'a leaders by doing so. "Closure eliminates a free vote," Calder said later. "With its house majority, the NDP would have been able to pass the treaty anyway. I wanted the treaty to be fully aired—under a free vote. Then the public would never call for a referendum." And the day after the treaty received approval from the BC Legislature, another vocal critic denounced the government's use of closure. In a letter to Lieutenant Governor Garde Gardom, Bill Vander Zalm, the president of the BC Reform Party, demanded that the "deceitful, damaging [treaty] document" be referred back to the legislature for full and complete debate.

Four days after the Nisga'a Treaty was ratified by the Canadian Senate, lawyers for BC Liberal leader Gordon Campbell and party members Geoffrey Plant and Mike de Jong appeared in Supreme Court in Vancouver to challenge the constitutionality of the agreement, claiming the treaty

Former Social Credit Premier William Vander Zalm, the outspoken treaty critic who ironically legitimized the Nisga'a treaty negotiations in 1990 when he ordered his officials to officially join the land claim talks.

entrenched a "third order" of government. Fighting the treaty at every stage, Gordon Campbell had first staked out his opposition at a party convention in November 1995, when he was asked by a *Globe and Mail* reporter what he would do about the Nisga'a Treaty when and if he were elected premier. He replied, "We will not respect a settlement that does not reflect the principal of 'one law for all British Columbians.'"

In this rare foray by politicians into the courts, the BC Liberals claimed the treaty enshrines a new order of government beyond the Constitution. They argued that because sovereign power is already fully distributed between Ottawa and the provinces, the Nisga'a Treaty contravenes the *Constitution Act*. To make it legal, they said, it requires a constitutional change and, under BC law, any constitutional change must pass a referendum. Since Victoria refused to hold a referendum on the treaty, the BC Liberals asked the court to set aside the treaty's unconstitutional provisions. They argued the Constitution doesn't allow Ottawa and Victoria to surrender that authority and that self-government cannot be granted in a treaty without amending the Constitution or passing separate legislation.

This argument had already been repeatedly dismissed by eminent legal experts such as Peter Hogg, Patrick Monahan and Bruce Ryder of Osgoode Hall Law School, who note that Section 35 was expressly amended in 1983 to include treaty rights "that now exist by way of land claims agreements or so may be required." Appearing before a Senate committee in Ottawa, Ryder had explained it this way: "The Nisga'a rights of self-government, rather than amounting to a constitutional amendment, have been acquired according to the very process contemplated by the constitutional amendments ratified by Canadian governments in 1982 and 1983."

Inside the Vancouver courtroom, these themes were embroidered before Justice Paul Williamson on behalf of the Nisga'a by lawyers Jim Aldridge and Thomas Berger, the former BC Supreme Court justice and longtime advocate of Nisga'a rights. Reserving his decision until late in the afternoon on July 24, 2000, Justice Williamson threw out the BC Liberal challenge in a 76-page decision. "I have concluded that after the assertion of sovereignty by the British Crown, and continuing to and after the time of Confederation, although the right of aboriginal people to govern themselves was diminished, it was not extinguished," he wrote. "Any aboriginal right to self-government could be extinguished after Confederation and before 1982 by federal legislation ... Post-1982, such rights cannot be extinguished, but they may be defined (given content) in a treaty. The Nisga'a Final Agreement does the latter expressly."

He found that the division of federal and provincial jurisdictions in 1867 did not cover everything. It didn't affect the continuing development of the common law. It didn't override the preamble to the Constitution, which indicated that many other powers and principles could be considered constitutional even if they weren't written down. And it didn't interrupt the royal prerogative, which continued after Confederation, of negotiating aboriginal treaties without Parliament's involvement. "The unique relationship between the Crown and aboriginal peoples, then, is an underlying constitutional value," the judge concluded. The BNA Act may have given the Parliament of Canada "exclusive legislative authority" over all matters involving "Indians and Lands reserved for Indians," but the only powers being divided were those that had been held by the provinces before Confederation. They didn't include powers held by the

Crown. In any case, Judge Williamson wrote, the Supreme Court of Canada has recognized that, although the treaty rights of the Nisga'a and other bands have constitutional protection, Parliament has the reserve power to interfere with any decisions the bands make *if* it can justify its interference in the name of the greater public good "consistent with the honour of the Crown."

The Liberal MLAs have other quarrels with the treaty, and with one issue in particular: the ineligibility of non-aboriginal residents on Nisga'a Lands to vote or run for Nisga'a councils remains a concern for many. But Judge Williamson compellingly argued that such battles must be fought elsewhere. As to the BC Liberals' claim that the denial of voting rights to non-Nisga'a living on Nisga'a territory contravenes the Charter of Rights and Freedoms, the court found that it is merely speculative since no one yet has actually been denied those rights. The judge pointed out that the treaty permits the Nisga'a government to grant citizenship to non-Nisga'a and he noted many Canadians already have their voting rights abridged by provincial residency requirements and laws and bylaws of municipalities and administrative boards. The Constitution, therefore, had made provision for everything Mr. Campbell argues against.

In dismissing the case, Justice Williamson ruled that aboriginal people have an inherent right to self-government—a right that cannot be extinguished. It is the first time that a court has acknowledged that. The judge also ruled that sovereign power was not fully exhausted between Parliament and the provincial legislatures. In other words, there is some residual power that could be distributed to aboriginal governments.

The ruling came as a major blow to the BC Liberal Party, which had hoped to strike down the treaty. On hearing news of his courtroom defeat, Campbell told reporters he would appeal the decision even if Williamson's persuasive ruling suggests that treaty opponents will find little traction when they appeal to the BC Court of Appeal and, perhaps, the Supreme Court of Canada. The next day, July 25, 2000, Campbell appealed.

Following the Nisga'a courtroom victory a briefing was held at the Chateau Granville Hotel for Gosnell and other Nisga'a leaders, at which time Berger said the judgement clarifies an important issue. "It explodes the myth that there is no such thing as a right of self-government," he said. "It's a judgement that upholds the importance of self-government in treaties. It makes it clear the rights are constitutionally protected. The message here is that aboriginal self-government was never extinguished...It survived Confederation." Said a smiling Gosnell as he emerged from the meeting, "I'm extremely pleased that we have now been vindicated by the Supreme Court. We've always said that we had the right to govern ourselves. Now that right has been upheld." Two months earlier, in an interview with *BC Business Magazine*, Gosnell had called Campbell "a dinosaur" and a direct link to William Smithe and Joseph Trutch, whose nineteenth-century policies doomed aboriginal people to a century of despair. It was clear to Gosnell that with Campbell as premier, relations with aboriginal people in British Columbia would be as glacial as the waters of Meziadin Lake.

During the 1990s the conflicts surrounding the treaty were always front page news in BC. During the period between 1991 and 1998, the *Province* and the *Vancouver Sun* published a combined total of 912 articles about the treaty, with both critics and supporters holding forth on the opinion pages.

And in July 1998 the *Sun* published a special series on the treaty. Two months later BC community newspaper mogul David Black (no relation to Conrad Black) ordered all his BC editors to oppose the Nisga'a Treaty. The Victoria-based businessman, whose fifty community newspapers in Western Canada and the US Pacific Northwest generate more than $150 million annually, said that the way senior governments were negotiating treaties was causing a racial divide that could cause bloodshed. "I think, if we don't solve it, we're going to create a Northern Ireland," Black told a reporter. "We're going to balkanize the province. We're going to have people shooting at each other."

To ensure his editors were singing from the same hymn book, Black held a "re-education camp" in the fall of 1998, where the late Mel Smith, QC—a former senior provincial civil servant, constitutional expert and anti-treaty author— delivered a seminar designed to make converts of Black's reporters and editors. Smith had come to public attention in 1991 when he wrote a report called *The Renewal of the Federation: A British Columbia Perspective*, but it was his 1995 book, *Our Home or Native Land?*, which made a frontal attack on the provincial government's treaty-making process, that brought him notice in BC. Arguing that provincial governments were giving too much land to aboriginal peoples, he opposed the granting of any rights—such as those related to land, fishing or logging—to aboriginal people based on their ethnicity. During the public debate over the treaty, he wrote several columns for David Black's newspapers dissecting what he described as flaws in the treaty.

As "balance" for his newspapers' editorials, Black solicited three op-eds from Premier Clark, three from Gordon Campbell, one from Bill Vander Zalm and one from Gordon

Wilson, then leader of the short-lived Progressive Democratic Alliance party. Another article carried a David Black byline. Most of the anti-treaty rhetoric plowed the same, well-turned soil, arguing that individual aboriginal people should receive treaty payments and individual parcels of land instead of what Black described as the "commune or communistic collective" set out in the treaty. "The ultimate goal should be the integration of aboriginal people with the rest of society," wrote Black, who was later hauled before the toothless BC Press Council, the self-policing tribunal set up to respond to media complaints.

Black's decree that all of his papers should oppose the treaty hit the staff of one of his papers especially hard. Throughout the years, few had watched the politics of the Nisga'a Treaty more closely than Rod Link and Jeff Nagel of *The Terrace Standard*, the newspaper published closest to Nisga'a territory, and as a result of its fair and thoughtful reporting, the *Standard* was seen locally as cautiously in favour of land claims. A "show-me" skeptic when it comes to reporting on the public affairs of the Terrace citizens—white or aboriginal—Link has always rejected the dewy-eyed romanticism projected by environmentalists and writers from urban centres, and he is a shrewd observer on the frontlines of "Indian Country," so that for him naive apotheosizing of either nature or aboriginal peoples has little currency. For Link, therefore, the Black mandate precipitated a career-defining ethical dilemma, tough irony for a man who had so

David Black, BC community newspaper mogul.
Glenn Baglo/Vancouver Sun, *1979*

judiciously guided his newspaper through the shoals of contention. Even though the *Standard* was not asked to skew its news coverage—nor did it—to the Black orthodoxy, Link would later concede that he did alter the paper's editorial pages to reflect his boss's edict. "It's not my newspaper," he admitted as his op-ed pages brimmed with anti-treaty rhetoric. An angry Gosnell could hardly contain himself. "So much for the ballyhooing of the media and the sacredness of the freedom of the press. Black is using his prestige and

Top: Nisga'a leader Rod Robinson being interviewed by *The Terrace Standard* reporter Jeff Nagel. *Gary Fiegehen photo*
Bottom: Rod Link, publisher-editor of *The Terrace Standard*. *Jeff Nagel photo*

wealth to oppose the treaty. What's next? Radio, television, corporations?"

Back east, Conrad Black's *National Post* had published seven consecutive anti-treaty opinion articles by the fall of 1999. The Nisga'a, having been successful in getting equal space with other newspapers—on par, most coverage supported the deal—phoned the *Post* to demand that their side of the story be told. Rebuffed, the Nisga'a then wrote several letters to the editor; these also went unpublished. Finally, on April 3, 2000, they contacted *Post* publisher Ken Whyte by e-mail, and he replied via the same medium, explaining the newspaper's stance: "We were dealing with legislation already written, and which had the support of the federal government. It was barrelling through the system without adequate thought to the consequences. We felt a duty to give it more scrutiny than it was receiving. We as a newspaper, on our editorial pages (as distinguished from our news columns), do not support Nisga'a." Drawing on his experience at *Alberta Reports* magazine, Whyte had already encouraged his conservative reporters to call into question the Charter of Rights and Freedoms, the notion of racial and sexual equality and, unfortunately for the Nisga'a, Canada's system of treaty making.

Another formidable treaty adversary was Thomas Flanagan, a professor of political science at the University of Calgary and former director of research for the Reform Party of Canada. A contributing *Post* columnist, as well as a consultant to the federal negotiating team, his views were given wide play by the *Post* during the debate on Parliament Hill. He argued that most of Canada's 625 aboriginal reserves are caught in a welfare trap, where the steady flow of public money saps individual incentive and perpetuates poverty. He also claimed the Nisga'a Treaty would set up a new order of government without any constitutional amendment.

Angered by the *Post*'s editorial stance and the opinions of columnists like Flanagan on the treaty, Gosnell and other tribal leaders fought back, pointing out the difference between the Nisga'a Treaty and the one described by critics. "The first is the treaty we negotiated," Gosnell told the House of Commons aboriginal affairs committee.

> It is the treaty being debated in the Commons. The other is a make-believe treaty, one that we never sought and would not accept if it were offered to us. It is the treaty described by the Official Opposition, the British Columbia Liberal party, and a variety of editorialists and other individuals. Among other supposed ills, the make-believe treaty would undermine the Charter of Rights, deny Nisga'a people the right to hold private property, hurt aboriginal women, allow the band to impose taxation without representation, and dramatically alter the Constitution. The Nisga'a treaty, the real Nisga'a treaty, does not do any of those things.

Criticism, however, continued at full volume. On newspaper opinion pages and on hotline radio, CKNW talk show host Rafe Mair weighed in against the deal. From the time the Nisga'a Agreement was first introduced in 1996, he had criticized the deal. He had also used his twice-weekly column in the *Vancouver Courier* as another anti-treaty vehicle, publishing a string of seventeen anti-treaty columns there over a ten-week period before he moved on to the *Province* for more of the same. But he apparently was not eager to face those he

had accused of perpetrating the treaty he condemned. On July 20, 1998, just two weeks before the treaty was initialled in Gitlakdamiks, when Nisga'a consultant Bob Spence accompanied Gosnell to the CKNW studios in Vancouver to appear on the Bill Good Show, he spotted Mair walking down the hall. When Mair saw Gosnell, Spence recalls, he looked embarrassed and did a quick about-face, darting into another office, leaving Spence with the impression that Mair would only fulminate to an empty studio or with like-minded guests, such as Gordon Campbell and Skeena Reform MP Mike Scott.

Despite being the MP who had represented the Nisga'a in Ottawa since 1993, Scott only once visited the Nass Valley, and he has made it clear that he mistrusts the Tribal Council. When he was re-elected to Parliament in the summer of 1997, an editorial in *The Terrace Standard* argued that it was time for him to mend fences with the Nisga'a. But Scott was not interested, and during the uproar prior to the initialling of the Nisga'a agreement-in-principle (precursor to the final treaty) he even warned that if negotiators concluded the deal that was on the table, there would be "social unrest like we've never seen before...Yes, by non-native

Top: Rafe Mair, Vancouver radio talk show host.
Bottom: Mike Scott, former Reform-Alliance MP for Skeena. Vancouver Sun

people. We are so close to violence in rural BC that it's not funny." Years earlier, he had sent off a letter for publication in Ottawa's parliamentary newsletter, the *Hill Times*, attacking proposed gun-control laws on the grounds that only an "armed citizenry" could defend itself against "those who seek unlimited power for government." When his remarks proved troublesome for party leader Preston Manning, Scott tried to tidy up the situation by claiming a staff member had authored the letter, but he later told Sterling news service he had several reasons to suspect a dictatorship could be in store for Canada, and it "certainly makes the government a lot more comfortable when they feel citizens are unarmed." Then, as if trying to set off another alarm bell, he added, "If we think we've seen problems at Oka or other parts of Canada with confrontation, we haven't seen anything yet. I'm not a scaremonger, but I hear it every day. It's frightening." It was, therefore, no surprise when Scott declined an invitation to appear at the 1999 Nisga'a annual convention held in Terrace, although it was being held mere blocks from his constituency office.

As the debate droned on in Ottawa, it became clear that some supporters and critics were engaged in a series of skilful distortions, made possible because few people had read the actual treaty. Because of its heft and labyrinthine complexity, many people who hadn't read the treaty used it as a blank slate upon which they projected their own hopes and fears, creating a polarized, hothouse atmosphere ill-suited to thoughtful analysis. Some weight was added to the pro side of the argument by individuals such as Peter Hogg, dean of Osgoode Hall, when he made a presentation to the House of Commons Committee via video conference call on November 23, 1999. He argued that the treaty would liberate the Nisga'a from the paternalism of the *Indian Act* and that the system of self-government that was to be set up was based on constitutionally protected treaty rights. However, many other moderate voices were drowned out by all the sound and fury.

Even some of those who did make it through the treaty's 252 pages remained skeptical of its self-government provisions. One of these was resource expert Peter Pearse, a former professor of forestry economics at the University of British Columbia and author of royal commission inquiries on fisheries and forest policies, who had publicly supported the treaty at critical times. He told the *Vancouver Sun* that the fisheries component of the treaty appeared sound and based on the sustainable conservation of Nass River salmon stocks. In the spring of 2000, Pearse also submitted a presentation to a parliamentary committee highly supportive of the treaty's forestry provisions. Even so, the longtime federal Liberal remained troubled by what he called "the potential for conflicts arising from the sweeping powers of Nisga'a self-government."

As debate over the treaty turned ugly on Parliament Hill, in November 1999 the Select Standing Committee on Aboriginal Affairs travelled to BC for hearings in Terrace, Smithers, Prince George, Victoria and Vancouver. (In a preemptive strike, Gordon Campbell was quick to label this hearing process "a sorry, pathetic excuse for democracy.")

Peter Pearse, West Coast resource economist.
Courtesy Peter Pearse

The first session held in Terrace on November 15 was benign and sparsely attended, perhaps because local residents, the nearest white neigbours to the Nisga'a, were suffering from "Nisga'a fatigue." About eighty people attended the session to hear local mayors carefully endorse the treaty, arguing that it will bring economic certainty to the region. "The people who are opposed to the treaty continue to behave in a condescending manner to the aspirations of the Nisga'a people," said Terrace mayor Jack Talstra. "They will tell the Nisga'a what should be in their treaty. That's not life in the 1990s." Prince Rupert mayor Jack Mussallem said his city also backed the deal, although concerns remained about its effects on the forest and fishing industries. "The majority of people are in favour of it," he said.

The only anti-treaty voice heard by the committee in Terrace was that of Frank Barton, a Nisga'a man born in Gingolx who now lived in Richmond. Barton maintained most of the Gingolx traditional lands didn't make it into the treaty because the village was "sold out" by the Nisga'a leadership who, he said, proceeded with the treaty and its ratification without proper internal authority. "I call it a modern-day robbery of land on the Gingolx people," Barton said. "This is not fair to the 1,700 band members of the Gingolx band."

The tone of the hearings changed dramatically the following day in Smithers when Gitanyow chief Glen Williams told the committee the Nisga'a Treaty amounted to an "act of aggression." He stated that, under the ratified treaty, 84 percent of what the Gitanyow claim as traditional territory is now within the Nisga'a core lands. "We believe the Nisga'a Final Agreement is an invasion to our birthright, our homeland," explained Gitanyow chief Darlene Vegh. "We won't go away and we won't stop fighting for our land." In addition, the committee heard from Gitksan representatives, who announced that even if the treaty were to be ratified, as was soon to be the case, the Gitksan were not going to let the Nisga'a trespass on their land. "I'm telling you, the tolerance level is going to be very low," warned Gitksan legal counsel Gordon Sebastian.

During one particularly heated exchange at the Prince George hearing on November 17, Mayne Island author Terry Glavin suggested to Reform MP Dick Harris that his party had "poisoned the public debate" over the treaty and that Reform was supported by "a small number of people who don't mind becoming the laughing stock of civilized countries." Harris shot back, "I guess we up here in Prince George have it all wrong, Mr. Glavin, so I'm glad you're here to put us straight." Asked by Harris how he felt about "taking time at these hearings away from the people of Prince George," Glavin replied, "I do not presume to come up to Prince George to tell people they are wrong. I believe my views are consistent with the vast majority of British Columbians." He referenced a series of Angus Reid polls showing that, throughout the 1990s, about 60 percent of Canadians supported the Nisga'a Treaty. In British Columbia, however, the polls indicated a dead heat, with supporters and opponents hovering near 40 percent and a huge number of undecided responses. The polls also confirmed that the number of supporters had dropped significantly once Premier Clark had wrapped himself in the treaty and personalized the deal for his own political purposes in the fall of 1998. While the tone of the hearing had been very unfriendly and combative to this point, it turned vicious when a man from the audience announced that one of the committee members, Nunavut

Liberal MP Nancy Karetak-Lindell, should "stop whining and go back to her reserve."

Skeena Reform MP Mike Scott, who attended all three of the sessions held in northwestern BC, suggested that the generally positive tone of the Terrace hearing had been largely due to the people there being uncomfortable about opposing the treaty. "People feel that regardless of what happens we're all neighbours here," he said, adding he hadn't expected open protests. "There's concern that the community is going to be able to stay united down the road." As for the Prince George hearing, he claimed it had been stacked with "treaty supporters and treaty apologists."

In Victoria, the committee heard delegations in an Empress Hotel meeting room. Among the presenters was Gordon Gibson Jr. who, with rhetorical flourishes, marched his audience through his anti-treaty themes to a dramatic ending during which he seemed to suggest he wanted to save individual Nisga'a people from foolish judges and skewed

Nancy Karetak-Lindell, Liberal MP (Nunavut) congratulates Edward Allen and other Nisga'a leaders after the treaty was passed by the House of Commons. *Gary Fiegehen photo*

federal policies. While he spoke, Frank Calder, an early hero of the Nisga'a quest, took notes in a desultory fashion; he had been hired to monitor the hearing and report back to Gosnell. At the Vancouver hearings, held in a meeting room of the Crowne Plaza Hotel on Georgia, populist politician Bill Vander Zalm, supported by a noisy Reform BC crowd, repeatedly disrupted pro-treaty submissions by BC Hydro chair Brian Smith and Simon Fraser University chancellor and investment banker Milton K. Wong. Ironically, it was Vander Zalm, the discredited Social Credit premier, who had legitimized the Nisga'a treaty negotiations in 1990, when he ordered provincial government officials to officially join land claim talks already underway between the Nisga'a and the federal government.

During the countdown to ratification, a curious Vancouver-based lobby group called CANFREE—Canadians for Reconciliation, Equality and Equity—emerged as a major backroom player among anti-treaty forces. According to national columnist Jim McNalty of the *Province*, lawyer John Weston, who fronts CANFREE, wouldn't reveal the names of the group's members to reporters, but in July 1999 he circulated a private letter to "Canadian Friends" listing names of people sympathetic to his cause. Among them were BC Liberal Geoff Plant; Gordon Campbell strategist Martyn Brown (a former Reform Party of Canada strategist); Mike Scott; Rafe Mair; Mark Milke of the Canadian Taxpayers Federation; lawyers

Gordon Gibson Jr., newspaper columnist and senior fellow at The Fraser Institute.
*Peter Blashill/*Vancouver Sun, *1993*

John Pitt and Harry Bell-Irving, and Gordon Gibson Jr. Later identified was Eric Sykes, formerly Alcan's president of BC operations in charge of the Kitimat smelter. In his letter, Weston stressed that "any movement that results from our deliberations ought not to be identified as the brainchild or tool of any political party."

CANFREE's members were instrumental in convincing former Supreme Court of Canada justice Willard Estey, age eighty, to testify before the Senate Standing Committee on Aboriginal Affairs on March 23, 2000. Estey's appearance—an exceedingly rare event for an ex-high court judge—seems to have been an act of desperation by anti-treaty forces, a last-ditch effort to halt the treaty. Like others before him, he argued the deal was unconstitutional. So did eighty-one-year-old Alex Macdonald, former BC Attorney General and major force in the provincial NDP of the 1970s, who testified on the same day, breaking ranks with his party to say that the treaty was unconstitutional. "It's a trap that will slam shut," he told the committee, revisiting a message he had tried to pitch to

The Nisga'a "war room" in the Minto Place Suite
Hotel, Ottawa. *Gary Fiegehen photo*

reporters when the parliamentary road show swept through Vancouver.

In Ottawa, meanwhile, as debate on Bill C-9 raged in the House of Commons, Gosnell brooded in the Nisga'as' makeshift "war room" in the Minto Place Suite Hotel. Supplied with phone lines, notebook computers, faxes and stacks of newspaper clippings, this room served as a communications command post for the Nisga'a team whose members spent most of each day in the public gallery of the House, it being their perception that if they were not a constant presence the treaty would never be ratified. Afterwards they would return to the room to hold briefings and plan the tactics for the next day of battle.

On December 13, 1999 the Liberal-controlled House of Commons passed the bill to ratify the treaty by a vote of 217–48, and the next day the bill was sent to the Senate for review. Rather than begin their deliberations then, the Senate promptly declared a Christmas break. The Nisga'a team, with nothing to keep them in Ottawa, also took a break, going home to the Nass Valley. But they were back in their war room by the time the Senate resumed sitting on February 8, 2000.

The basic decency and good humour of the Nisga'a team was put to its ultimate test during that final vigil on Parliament Hill. The ordeal had simply taken too long for a group defined by its implacable patience. "It's shameful and inexcusable, all these delays," admitted one federal official in a moment of candour. Tempers frayed as the Nisga'a leaders

Willard Estey, former Supreme Court of Canada justice. *Ralph Bower/*Vancouver Sun got on each other's nerves. A few "got lost" at the hotel bar. There was waiting and yet more waiting for the Nisga'a team as the Senate, with its inexplicable schedule, plodded through its deliberations.

Gosnell, never much of a television viewer, would amble into the war room on Sunday afternoons to slope into a chair and stare blankly at televised hockey and basketball as he tried to unwind. He took time to attend a seminar at a university in Ontario, where he explained to law and history students the background to the landmark debate. This visit, besides being a much-needed distraction, showed Gosnell at his best; his regal bearing and relaxed manner made him popular with the students. But in other settings he could smoulder with a righteous anger that more accurately reflected his frame of mind at this point. After a session at Queen's University in Kingston on February 10, 2000, a Canadian Press reporter waited in the hall to ask for comment on the latest Reform attack on the treaty. "We've heard this all before," Gosnell thundered, "about how dreadful this is all going to be. Let me turn the tables on the Reform MPs. Do they really want to stay with the Indian reserve system, which is what we've had all these many years? Do they really want us to remain wards of the state, beggars in our own lands?" Days later, Gosnell powerfully enhanced this theme when he told a visiting German television documentary team about the destructiveness of the status quo, about the suicides, alcohol and drug abuse, domestic violence, despair and nihilism that plague some of his people. "I think it's important for this committee and other Canadians to recognize this current system we're living under, which is the *Indian Act*, directed by the Department of Indian Affairs. It's important for Canadians to recognize this Act was imposed upon aboriginal people. We played no part whatsoever in devising or adding to its contents, never. Right from the start, Ottawa deemed it necessary, for whatever reasons that came to them, to impose that Act on our people. Today, we're still living under that Act."

One night in April, a guitar appeared in the war room. Aldridge and others took turns strumming through a series of basic chord changes before it ended up in the hands of Nisga'a communications coordinator Eric Grandison, a shy man who spent long hours in his own company. Warming up with a series of diatonic blues scales, he flat-picked his way through several signature Albert King turnarounds—the classic licks copied by a generation of rock musicians—before taking off on an impressive display of fretboard virtuosity. Rocking gently, he closed his eyes and seemed to fall into a trance as the music poured spontaneously from him. He loved music, lived for music, used music as solace for the vicissitudes of his own life which, like the songs of the bluesmen he worshipped, had been steeped in suffering and hard times. He told me that back in Gitlakdamiks, one wall of his tiny home was lined with more than 2,000 CDs and 3,000 LPs, mostly rock and blues, while across the room, a Takemine acoustic guitar took pride of place. "One day," he said, "I'd like to write a song about the treaty, a simple twelve-bar blues with lots of room to improvise, go ballistic. Maybe I'll call it the Treaty Blues."

After two months of sporadic stop-start deliberations, the Liberal-controlled Senate ratified the treaty on April 13, 2000, by a vote of 52–15. Moments later a tired but jubilant Gosnell was surrounded by his Nisga'a colleagues and white supporters: "It's taken us 113 years to get here, 113 years to settle the land question. We're simply finishing the work of our ancestors," he said before the weary colleagues set off to celebrate

at an Italian restaurant near the University of Ottawa. Five thousand miles away, notified by telephone, the Nisga'a people rushed into the unpaved streets of their villages to cheer and wave small Canadian flags. Backdropped by the four sacred mountains that ring the Nass River Valley, the fluttering Maple Leaf flags made real the long years of the Nisga'a people's struggle to join Canada as free and equal citizens.

But while the Nisga'a celebrated, the treaty's opponents licked their wounds and reassessed their futures. On August 9, 2000, Scott surprised the citizens of Terrace when he announced he would not run for re-election when Chrétien dissolves Parliament. The Canadian Alliance (formerly Reform) MP said he made the decision for personal reasons. "I was thirty-nine when I was first elected and I'm forty-six now," said Scott. "I do have commitments out there to meet and these are considered in life to be the prime earning years." He gave no immediate indication of how he would make a living after leaving public office but warned it is "a

Prime Minister Chrétien, Phil Fontaine (centre), National Chief of the Assembly of First Nations, and two ministers congratulate Chief Gosnell following passage of the treaty in the House of Commons. *Nisga'a Archives* mistake for anyone to consider politics as a career." In an interview with *The Terrace Standard*, Scott vociferously defended his criticisms of the treaty claiming it constitutionally entrenches a third order of government. "It was very regrettable we were not able to be more successful in having the Nisga'a Treaty go to referendum in BC," said Scott. "It wasn't for lack of trying. We were up against a pretty powerful status quo. I'm proud of what we did despite being portrayed personally in very unflattering terms and to be portrayed as having really despicable motives and have my character dragged through the mud." He said he was worn down from taunts from political opponents who accused him of being a racist.

"My personal faith in the entire political process has been badly shaken," he told *Vancouver Sun* Ottawa bureau chief Peter O'Neil. He conceded that he remains upset that many municipal politicians and business leaders in his riding privately encouraged his battle against the treaty but refused to take a public stand. "I don't want to paint everybody with the same brush, but there were a lot of people in this riding who were concerned about their businesses and their prospects of maintaining business relationships with native people. There were people who in my opinion knew better but would not stand up and be counted."

A bitterly disappointed Scott then took a "holiday" from politics and absented himself from the caucuses of the Canadian Alliance, which had taken over from Reform. His new leader, Stockwell Day, however, warned Scott on September 19, 2000, to either show up regularly for work or consider leaving politics. Day added that Scott's situation points to the need for legislation to allow constituents to recall MPs who don't fully perform their duties.

CHAPTER NINE:

The Neighbours

There's a popular joke on British Columbia's North Coast about two men—one aboriginal, one white—who are catching crabs at the end of a pier. The white man has a lid on his crab pot to keep the crabs from scrambling out; the aboriginal fisher does not and is asked why. "Mine are Indian crabs," he says. "Whenever one climbs to the top to escape, the others drag it back down."

The joke has a certain relevance to the Nisga'a negotiations. On November 7, 1998, more than 72 percent of eligible Nisga'a voters approved the treaty that Gosnell and the Nisga'a team had negotiated, and the document was sent down to Victoria for debate. But embarrassing to Gosnell and his team, a small group from Gingolx tried to derail the

Nass River, just above Lakalzap.
Gary Fiegehen photo

deal, claiming they had not been appropriately represented on the 32-member Nisga'a negotiating team and angry that more of their wilps had not been officially protected as core lands under the treaty. In May, 1998, Frank Barton and James Robinson, formerly of Gingolx, launched a court challenge to the treaty, alleging that the Nisga'a negotiators did not have the authority of their people. This was dismissed by the BC Supreme Court in July, 1998, and a subsequent appeal was also dismissed. In the spring of 2000, Barton and Robinson apparently hired lawyer and CANFREE organizer John Weston to prepare yet another court challenge.

This rift underscores the heated emotions and age-old rivalries between villages. Under the treaty, the Nisga'a Lands were pared down to less than 2,000 square kilometres from the 24,000-plus square kilometres they had claimed as traditional territory. Faced with the dilemma of which lands would be included in this small territory, the team made the decision to protect lands in the central Nass Valley; other lands, especially those near Gingolx, were taken off the table. This, of course, was the harsh reality of the negotiations, described by Gosnell as "a hard-fought compromise." Right to the end, however, many Nisga'a negotiators continued to believe that significantly more than the 2,000 square kilometres would be designated as core lands in the final treaty, and it was agonizingly painful for some of the chiefs to accept the inevitability that their traditional wilps had been unprotected.

But there was trouble with the tribal neighbours as well. Less than three weeks after debate began on the Nisga'a Treaty in the British Columbia Legislature, the Gitanyow announced that the treaty was "an act of aggression," and went to court to argue that the federal and provincial governments had been negotiating with them in bad faith. The

Sganisim Xhlaawit (Vetter Peak), one of four sacred
mountains in Nisga'a territory. *Gary Fiegehen photo*

Gitanyow occupy the territory west of the Kispiox River and north of the Skeena, sandwiched between the powerful Nisga'a and the equally powerful Gitksan, to whom they are culturally related but from whom they are fiercely independent. The reason for their court challenge was that in the territory north of Kitwanga along Highway 37 some of the land and hunting rights that the Gitanyow were claiming in their negotiations with the government had been ceded to the Nisga'a. At the same time, the Gitksan, who live just east and north of the Gitanyow, also complain that another 9,053 square kilometres—about 32 percent of the lands over which they claim traditional jurisdiction—have also been included in Nisga'a management zones.

With the ratification of the treaty, the Nisga'a now control a share of the fishery on the entire Nass, including portions of the river that pass through both Gitanyow and Gitksan traditional territories. As well, the Nisga'a are guaranteed a hunting entitlement in an area covering much of the Nass watershed, including Gitanyow territory. While it is true that when treaties have been concluded with the Gitksan and Gitanyow peoples, these hunting and fishing rights will be shared with the two groups, it doesn't make it any easier for them to swallow in the meantime. Another of their key objections is the selection by the Nisga'a of a number of fee simple sites—small plots of land away from the Nisga'a core lands—which may be suitable for various kinds of economic development. Some of the best of these sites for fishing and other opportunities, according to Gitanyow hereditary chief Glen Williams, are within Gitanyow traditional territory. This overlap issue is even more complicated than it appears on the surface because of the migrations and interconnectedness of some families; some of the people living in Gitlakdamiks, for example, have family ties to Gitanyow. An ancient Nisga'a insult, in fact, is to tell someone to "go back home to Gitanyow."

The two tribes offer a study in contrast. The Nisga'a are widely perceived as moderates, principled and, above all, deeply committed to the formal process of land claims. "We want to negotiate our way into Canada," Gosnell repeatedly told reporters, emphasizing a key tribal council message. They have history on their side as well. Who could deny the mythology, the compelling power of a group that petitioned Victoria and London a century earlier seeking redress? A group that in 1891 published the newspaper, *Hagaga*, initially in the Nisga'a language, as a vehicle for the discussion of the land question? A tribe whose landmark Calder Case initiated the modern process of treaty making?

The Gitanyow, on the other hand, use confrontational tactics and inflammatory rhetoric. Gitanyow chief Williams charges that, under the Nisga'a Treaty, the government is granting the Nisga'a rights they never owned historically. "The Nisga'a treaty represents a major assault against our laws, against our system," he says. "It's the supreme violation of the *ayuukhl* [traditional code of law]. The punishment for that is mourning and then an outbreak of hostilities. Some of our people are pretty pissed, especially the older people. They are mad at the Nisga'a and the government both. They want to knock down some bridges on roads that are on the boundary." Continuing in the quasi-military language that defines his style, he warns of impending violence. "People are so very angry. It's such a big assault. They [the Gitanyow people] are going to get out there and exercise the fishing rights that they enjoyed without the presence of the Nisga'a in the past. We will occupy our land and we will not leave." Chafing from a sense of betrayal by senior governments in Ottawa and Victoria, in May 2000 Williams promised a series of court actions, one planned for February 2001, to seek a court declaration that the senior governments, upon entering negotiations with the Nisga'a, breached their responsibility to negotiate in good faith and protect Gitanyow interests.

This inter-tribal jousting has played into the hands of white treaty critics who, on the opinion pages and on radio talk shows, revelled in the news. If aboriginal peoples could not come to agreements between themselves, what were the chances for government negotiators? Overlaps, critics argued, were symptomatic of an ailing treaty-making process predicated on anti-assimilation policy assumptions. University of Victoria associate dean of arts and law professor Hamar Foster, a long-time supporter of the Nisga'a Treaty, suggests the failure to resolve the Gitanyow overlap tarnishes an otherwise fair and moderate treaty. "[This treaty] is also, by any reasonable standard, a good one [deal]," he wrote in BC *Studies* magazine. "This does not mean that it is a perfect agreement or even the best in the circumstances. As a product of human negotiation, it naturally has flaws; and although there is unlikely to be a consensus on what these are, one is certainly the failure to resolve the overlap issue between the Nisga'a and their neighbours, the Gitanyow."

However, overlaps are evidence of the fact that some territories were traditionally shared between neighbouring First Nations or that two or more First Nations held access rights to different resources on the same lands. Within this kind of overlap can also be found the happenstance of history. For example, a tribal council identifies the territory of the tribe in documents filed with the British Columbia Treaty

Commission. But within that tribe is an "Indian band" that ended up separated from its original tribal administration because of a long-forgotten decision by an Indian Affairs bureaucrat who was motivated solely by administrative efficiency. This Indian band then files its own treaty negotiation documents. The result is an apparent overlap by one First Nation's claim of 100 percent of the territory claimed by another First Nation. Other overlaps are at least partly the result of the stubborn petulance and hubris of some aboriginal leaders.

Because of the current configuration of the treaty-making process, aboriginal claims overlap each other throughout the entire province, creating a complicated and surreal mélange that has to be untangled in court. This could take years, even decades, because each aboriginal group stakes out its first, best position when entering the BC Treaty Commission process, hoping for as much land and cash as possible, even if, as is often the case, its claim overlaps with another. This is done in spite of the full knowledge that the tribe is very unlikely to receive more than 5 percent of the land claimed. As a result, while the claimants wait for treaty negotiations, tempers simmer, as both or all—sometimes there are three or more sides in a particular overlap dispute—frame their arguments and pitch their views to the media. And each new complexity raises the issue to the level of incomprehensible abstraction, dooming the debate to a seemingly pointless spiral.

That overlaps are a very real condition of aboriginal title in British Columbia and have always been so was recognized by the Supreme Court of Canada in its 1997 judgement, *Delgamuukw v. the Queen*. In their decision, the judges noted that a necessary condition of aboriginal title was proof of

Treaty Creek, the physical boundary between
Nisga'a and Tahltan territory. *Gary Fiegehen photo*

"exclusive" ownership by a First Nation, but recognizing the complexity of these issues, they also made allowance for something called "shared exclusivity," which allows two or more First Nations to continue to hold title to the same land, according to customary law. In some instances therefore, overlaps, far from being an expression of traditional conflict, may be seen as evidence of a history of peaceful co-existence between First Nations.

The Nisga'a treaty negotiations were encumbered by both the reality and the public perception of overlapping claims with their neighbours, the Gitksan, the Tsimshian and the Gitanyow. In the case of the Tsimshian, however, a straight-forward resolution of an apparent overlap in the lower reaches of the Nass River was concluded by direct negotiations between the two groups. In the case of the Gitksan and the Gitanyow, no such resolution has yet been possible.

To the outside world, the row over tiny plots of land in the Nass Valley takes on the appearance of a family feud, bred in the bone. After all, these are people whose ancestors for centuries back lived, worked and married along the same reaches of the Nass River and its tributaries. But over time, ancient slights have been magnified into a kind of grudge match, formalized today in parliamentary hearings, court actions and media campaigns. There are historic precedents for some of this animosity, anthropologists suggest, documenting an age of hand-to-hand combat where tribal warriors fought pitched battles dressed in wooden armour wound with whale gut. Kenneth Ames and Herbert Maschner, in their book *Peoples of the Northwest Coast: Their Archaeology and Prehistory*, write, "[In ancient times] wars continued even without competition for the basics of every-day life, either because old wounds truly do never heal and revenge wars are difficult to stop, or more likely, the act of war was so intricately woven into Northwest Coast systems of wealth, status and prestige that, regardless of the changing circumstances, the maintenance of rank through aggression was such a social institution that it was difficult to abandon."

Just prior to treaty ratification, a Senate committee, "deeply concerned about the implications of outstanding overlap issues," urged the Nisga'a to resolve the problem. The Nisga'a response was lukewarm, puzzling many, even their ardent supporters. Publicly, Gosnell emphasizes a willingness to meet with the Gitanyow but only in the company of a government-appointed mediator. This response from a leader whose "high-road" reputation is based on moderation leaves the uncomfortable impression that the Nisga'a juggernaut with its superior legal firepower and public relations machine might be willing to roll over the aspirations of other tribal neighbours if they get in their way.

Saul Terry, head of the Union of BC Indian Chiefs and long-time critic of the BC Treaty Commission process, raised the Nisga'a overlap issue in an August 1998 editorial in the aboriginal newspaper *Kahtou*:

> The Gitanyow people, as a part of the Gitk'san Nations have experienced first hand the dishonour of the crown as demonstrated in the land overlap issue. This has exposed the Canadian treaty policy of first come, first served. In this way other communities or Nations are being strategically forced to the treaty table or as in the Gitanyow case to the court to defend their infringed upon Title. One must conclude that this is just another reason not to be involved in

this sham of a scheme. In retrospect, to paraphrase a saying after the holocaust of Jewish people: Where were we when they took the lands of the James Bay Cree? Where were we when they took the homelands of the Yukon Peoples? Now that they are coming to take a Nation's land and resources in our own back yard, where are we?

All of this animosity between northern First Nations deeply concerns their white neighbours in the town of Terrace, just 100 kilometres south of Nisga'a territory, for although Terrace city planners tout the city's new and diversified economy with its tax breaks and other incentives for small business and its ecotourism opportunities, a short drive past the city limits more accurately points out the real engine of the region's economy: logging. And the future of the logging

Lower Nass River below Fishery Bay, site of the eulachon fishery every March. *Gary Fiegehen photo*

industry is bound up inextrica-
bly with relations with their
aboriginal neighbours.

Forest industry production
represents about 34 cents of
every dollar of income here,
making it by far the region's
largest industry. Indeed, the
story of post-war Terrace can be
told through the rising fortunes
of several pioneering white
families who began the cutting
and milling of the huge conifer
forests of the region, building a
wealthy and powerful lobby
whose money helped to elect
officials sympathetic to logging,
mining and other resource

extraction. The logging industry moved into the Nass River
Valley in earnest forty years ago, making millionaires of at
least one successful family of logging contractors, Don Hull
& Sons Contracting.

Such fortunes are a source of impotent frustration and
painful embarrassment to the Nisga'a leadership, who were
unable to stop the logging while the treaty talks were underway. Despite a series of angry tirades, alternating with desperate pleadings, the provincial government refused to
adopt a system of "interim measures" to halt the logging.
This "talk-and-log" reality became what the Nisga'a call a
"chainsaw massacre" of the Nass forests and resulted in
clear-cuts as large as 6,000 hectares. One internal Nisga'a
study estimated that each year during the twenty-three years

Logging activity along the Stewart-Cassiar Highway
in Nisga'a territory. Meziadin Lake can be seen
at top left. *Gary Fiegehen photo*

Massive clear-cut adjacent to Gitlakdamiks.
Non-Nisga'a forest companies logged clear-cuts
as large as 6,000 hectares. *Gary Fiegehen photo*

of the negotiations, 30,000 truckloads, worth $60 million, were harvested from Nass forests. Another report concluded that 36,000 hectares had been inadequately reforested, and a Price Waterhouse study conducted in the 1980s estimated that this logging represented $2 billion of lost economic opportunity for the Nisga'a.

The Nass forests had been relatively untouched until 1948, when the British Columbia government granted Tree Farm Licence No. 1, covering 335,000 hectares, to Columbia Cellulose, an American company, on the condition that it build a pulp mill in the region. A second licence was added a few years later. The company met its obligations by establishing a bleached sulfite mill at Port Edward, near Prince Rupert, then left British Columbia in 1979. The mill, by then antiquated and unprofitable, and the forest tenures were taken over by a Crown corporation that eventually became Westar Timber. Over the years, much of the mature forest of

Staging area for non-Nisga'a logging operation.
Gary Fiegehen photo

both licences was logged out by local contractors like the Hulls. The Nisga'a people were never consulted about the licences or any other provincial government forestry decisions, and their people were rarely employed in the industry as the forest base disappeared. The leadership cites this as one of the reasons young people drifted away from the valley to seek jobs and income in cities to the south.

All that has changed. Under the treaty, the Nisga'a are the forests' owners, although the allowable annual cut (AAC) will still be regulated by BC's forestry department. For the first five years after signing, the volume of timber to be harvested will remain at a level somewhat lower than that in the immediately preceding years, and that volume will decline over the next four years. To ensure a continued flow of fibre for local mills, the cut for the first three years will be apportioned among the present licence holders, but they will receive a smaller portion over years four and five. Licences currently held by non-Nisga'a will expire by or before the end of this transition period, after which all timber on the Nisga'a Lands will be harvested by the Nisga'a or on their behalf. These rules, however, apply only to those portions of Nisga'a Lands that were not Indian reserves before the treaty; the Nisga'a are free to determine the harvest level on former reserve lands.

The Council of Forest Industries objected to the agreement on the grounds that it expropriated current licence holders without a clear indication of compensation. Therefore, they suggested that any reduction of production or obligatory closure of operable mills due to loss of fibre might be cause for a claim if one of these could demonstrate that it was induced to build mills, roads, and other establishments by the conditions of their earlier tenures. However, the licence holders in this case are mills such as Westar, and the agreement stipulates that the Nisga'a cannot enter into competition with the local mills for the next ten years.

The treaty also requires all current licensees to use Nisga'a contractors for timber harvesting on Nisga'a Lands. During the first year of the transition period, licensees will have to allocate half, and at a later date 70 percent, of their logging to Nisga'a contractors. This allocation was already happening to a certain extent before the effective date, said Nisga'a Lands and Resources Director Collier Azak, who helped to negotiate the forestry component of the treaty. He explained that several Gitlakdamiks-based contractors have been working for Skeena Cellulose for some time, and that number is expected to grow to four or five in 2000. The transition period will also allow time for more Nisga'a people to be trained to manage and work in the forestry industry, and he hopes

that now-underemployed Nisga'a people will fill the fifty or so full-time contracting positions currently held by non-aboriginals on their lands. In the meantime the government has hired a professional forester, and the forestry department has begun the huge job of administering forestry operations on Nisga'a land.

While the Nisga'a may conduct value-added timber processing, enter into partnerships with owners of existing facilities, or provide lumber for their

Nisga'a faller working on the lower Nass River, salvaging an area of blowdown. *Gary Fiegehen photo* own residential and public purposes, they have agreed not to build a sawmill for ten years. However, after that time, they intend to build a mill that could yield fifty to eighty more new jobs. From his office in the new Nisga'a Lisims Government Building, Azak scopes out the future of the Nass forests. "After the [five-year] transition period it's up to us. The forests here belong to Nisga'a people."

Naturally, in Terrace and other local lumber towns, there is anxiety about how the new landlords are going to treat logging contractors, loggers and millworkers. And while there has been near universal support from environmentalists for the treaty, there has been a back-channel debate about which environmental standards the Nisga'a might apply in their forest stewardship. These concerns are explained away by Azak, who points to a clause in the treaty which stipulates the Nisga'a must meet or beat all existing forest and environmental standards. A friendly and efficient man, he grows impatient with this kind of question. "We have been remarkably generous in our undertakings in the forest. When forest companies first came here, they were under no constraints and had little incentive to employ Nisga'a workers. They hit the Nass River forests at hurricane strength. That is changing today."

Indeed it is. Today, under the treaty, Nass River forests are still being cut and driven to sawmills in Terrace, but the logs bear the timber marks of the new Nisga'a Lisims Government. And for the first time money is beginning to flow back to the Nisga'a. The current harvesting rate of 165,000 cubic metres per year of wood, at a treaty-guaranteed stumpage rate of $6 per cubic metre—well over the current stumpage of less than $1—will channel nearly $1 million per year into the new Nisga'a government's general revenue.

The Nisga'a may over time build new relationships with their white neighbours in towns such as Terrace and Prince Rupert. An equal but different way of looking at the "other" is bound to emerge, a new clay to reshape the contours of a cruel and ragged history. It is one thing to have a legal document; quite another to have the goodwill of one's neighbour.

Majestic Sganisim Xhlaawit in central Nass Valley.
Gary Fiegehen photo

CHAPTER TEN

The Aftermath

O n September 14, 2000, in the village of
Gitlakdamiks, Joseph Gosnell and a procession of Nisga'a Lisims Government officials,
chiefs and elders paraded slowly across the
mica slate floor in the Great Hall of the new Wilpsi'ayuukhl
Nisga'a, the new legislative building. Then, to mark the opening of the assembly, matriarchs from the four clans—Killer
Whale, Eagle, Wolf and Raven—sliced a seven-metre-long
strip of cedar bark into pieces to be distributed to the guests.
They were followed by four chiefs who, in a traditional ceremony, shouted out the name of the building, after which the
doors of the legislature were thrown open for the Nisga'a
people to tour its halls as their leaders, all dressed in dark
business suits, looked proudly on. Guests included Bill

Aerial view of Old Aiyansh. *Gary Fiegehen photo*

Hartley, speaker of the BC Legislature, Energy Minister Dan Miller and NDP MLAs Bill Goodacre (Bulkley Valley-Stikine) and Helmut Giesbrecht (Skeena). The federal government was represented by Liberal MPs John Finlay (Oxford) and long-time Nisga'a supporter David Iftody (Provencher). Bloc Québécois Native Affairs Critic Claude Bachand and Senator Willie Adams from Nunavut were also on hand. Australian Supreme Court Justice John Onley, an aboriginal land commissioner, had travelled the farthest. First Nations guests included Richard Watts of the Nuu-chah-nulth Tribal Council, Chief Nancy Soudy of the Shuswap Nation and Chief Antoine Archie of the Canim Lake Band.

A jubilant tone pervaded the impressive two-storey structure of cedar siding and arched clerestory windows.

Master of ceremonies Kevin McKay opens
Wilpsi'ayuukhl Nisga'a in Gitlakdamiks,
September 14, 2000. *Gary Fiegehen photo*

Designed by the North Vancouver architectural firm of David Nairne & Associates, the building evokes the traditional Nisga'a longhouse, although it houses a complex of modern offices including the "oval office" of the president.

Here, in the new seat of government, Nisga'a politicians will decide how to invest the $196.1 million gained by the treaty as they try to build a new economy from the forests and fisheries of the Nass River Valley. To non-aboriginal observers the sum of money seems impressive, and it has been a lightning rod for anger across the province. But closer scrutiny reveals the limits of Nisga'a financial freedom. For one, there is the cost of negotiations—a $51.3 million loan to be repaid to the federal government within fifteen years. There is also the cash payout of $4.5 million as each of the three hundred Nisga'a elders, sixty years or older,

From left: federal negotiator Tom Molloy with MPs
David Iftody (Liberal) and Claude Bachand (Bloc)
at the opening of Wilpsi'ayuukhl Nisga'a.
Gary Fiegehen photo

receives a one-time $15,000 payment. As well, there will be another round of legal bills to fight the appeal that Gordon Campbell and the BC Liberals filed after losing in BC Supreme Court in July 2000. Should Campbell and company lose again, it is very likely the case will end up in the Supreme Court of Canada in Ottawa, adding yet more to the mounting courtroom bill.

Economist Roslyn Kunin of the Vancouver think-tank, the Laurier Institution, has expressed the hope that Nisga'a leaders will develop an investment policy to protect the $196.1 million trust fund, emphasizing the critical need "for tribal leaders to distinguish between capital and income." Nor does she mince words when offering her prescription for higher education in the Nass: "I am very concerned that, at present, the Nisga'a people do not have the educational requirements to succeed in the twenty-first century. There is a dearth of professional trained people such as foresters. To set this right, Nisga'a children must be encouraged to stay in school and Nisga'a adults should enroll in upgrading courses—now."

School District 92 (Nisga'a) chair Esther Adams agrees. Identifying the critical need for better education, she has worked overtime for the past ten years to help students stay in school in order to break the cycle of poverty and social dysfunction. In the spring of 2000 she delivered a rousing speech to the graduating class at

Esther Adams, Nisga'a entrepreneur and school board chair. *Jeff Nagel photo*

Nisga'a Senior High School in Gitlakdamiks, exhorting the graduates to help build an entrepreneurial climate in the Nass Valley. Running through a list of potential small business ventures—one-hour photo development, dry cleaning, automotive services, dry goods, courier and transportation services—she paused to emphasize an important caveat: "The success of your business will depend entirely on the amount of time and energy you put into it. Whatever your choice, risk-taking, commitment, sacrifice and foresight will be the constants." What Adams did not tell the graduates is that the failure rate for aboriginal businesses is astronomical. Much of this is due to the fact that most businesses depend on local market forces—population size, per capita and disposable income, spending habits and the like—and the client base for aboriginal businesses is generally limited to their own community. As a result, they face longer odds in starting a business than entrepreneurs in the general population. But challenging the students, Adams warned that they will have to adapt to the sometimes pitiless market forces of the world outside the Nass Valley: the fast-moving, post-Internet economy based on individual rights and free market capitalism.

She is backed by former negotiator Rod Robinson, who now sits behind a desk in the Wilpsi'ayuukhl Nisga'a as the new chairman of the Council of Elders. Hobbled by diabetes, insulin-dependent, the old warrior lives one day at a time, following a strict regime of pills and needles. Though he recently recovered from a serious bout of pneumonia that affected his heart and still requires medication, old age also affords him time for reflection and talking with young people in the streets of the village. Urging them to stay in school and attend college and other post-secondary institutions, he says, "The day will come when we will have our own doctors,

Nisga'a students climb into the school bus.
Gary Fiegehen photo

teachers and marine biologists. We have to. Under the treaty, we are now competing with the outer world, with all the people of Canada."

Esther Adams concluded her speech to the graduating class of 2000 by pointing a critical finger at the various "experts and consultants" that the Nisga'a government now employs, a loaded subject that rankled the graduates, many of whose mothers and fathers resent paying white lawyers, technicians and other specialists, even though at present few Nisga'a people have these skills. In this Adams was echoing one of Frank Calder's themes. "Over the years, we always said that under self-government we would rid ourselves of the *Indian Act* and all its officials," Calder said. "That means we have to run things ourselves. What I don't want is for us to substitute a system of 'consultants' government.' This is one of the downfalls of the whole treaty-making process. There are far too many white people in the negotiations rooms; too many of our own people don't know their own history. They haven't taken the time to actually learn about it."

Meanwhile, Esther Adams does more than talk about entrepreneurship. A slim, small-boned woman who looks much younger than her forty years, she brims with zeal for the photocopying business she started, using a $50,000 grant from Aboriginal Business Canada and a $30,000 loan from the aboriginal First Citizens Fund. She recently purchased two Canon machines—one a colour copier, the other a publishing unit—that can be linked to a network of personal computers. The hardware, now sitting on her basement floor, will soon be moved to a new storefront operation. In 1998 her one-person operation grossed earnings of $30,000; by the end of next fiscal year, she is expected to reach $90,000 and will need to hire two new staff.

In a rush, Nisga'a children clamber down the steps
of the old Community Hall. *Gary Fiegehen photo*

But while the Nisga'a are looking forward, beyond the Nass Valley critics have continued to attack the deal. In a *Post* opinion piece three days after the BC Liberal's courtroom defeat on July 24, 2000, Gordon Gibson Jr. called the judges in the case "foolish" for their decision. "The Nisga'a judgement of BC Supreme Court Judge Paul Williamson gives new nourishment to a nasty little cancer in Canadian society. That cancer would be the idea that political rights may be assigned on the basis of race or heritage—to aboriginals, in this case. This idea is always wrong, whether it leads to the well-intentioned policies yielding desperate results for the native underclass in Canada, or more carefully designed schemes of oppression elsewhere. But in BC we also live with reality, which is that our land and resource law is in a turmoil because of aboriginal claims."

Gibson is not alone in this view. Throughout the province there is a strong current of opinion that argues that the past is past, and modern generations are not obliged to set right the sins of their fathers. Some, insisting that governments are proceeding where they have no historical or legal obligation to do so, practise a flat and angry denial. Others refuse to admit there is a connection between the realities of the past and the grievances of the present. As if to say history is irrelevant, they argue that dwelling on decisions made one hundred years ago simply prevents aboriginal peoples from addressing the serious problems that they face today.

Historian Robin Fisher agrees that many British Columbians remain ignorant of their own history, and he blames professional historians like himself for the malaise. In a sweeping *mea culpa*, Fisher tars with the same brush the "specialists in native land claims" for their unwillingness to explain complex abstractions such as aboriginal title and aboriginal rights to the media and a confused and anxious general public. Little wonder, he says, that treaty making remains an insider's game—a closed and secret world where, huddled behind hotel doors, negotiators discourse with each other in the coded and legalistic parlance of their craft, while a skeptical public fumes on the sidelines. At the same time, he points out that treaty making is currently the most viable way to settle Canada's Indian Question. "When I think of the treaty process in British Columbia, I am reminded of Winston Churchill's remarks about democracy. The treaty process may not be perfect, indeed it may be the worst way to resolve the issue 'except for all those other forms that have been tried from time to time.' Those who wish for the failure of the treaty process should think of the alternatives and the consequences. It is the only means we have found of resolving the issues of land and government in this province in one hundred and fifty years."

First Nations policy in Canada has tended to lurch from one cure-all to another, from Christianization to residential schools to reserves to assimilation. To solve the "Indian Question" federal governments have sought to develop strategies and programs that would solve the social, economic and cultural difficulties facing First Nations communities, but with little success. The past thirty years have seen many of these attempts, from costly and unproductive programs of limited community self-government to highly promoted aboriginal economic development schemes. Few achieved the desired result. First Nations communities were not empowered, economic difficulties did not disappear, social problems were not solved. As well, critics began to complain, more loudly and persistently than in the past, that vast amounts of government funds—the annual DIAND budget

is now $6 billion—were being spent with little return on the taxpayers' investment. Indeed, the federal government has staked so much political capital—it is, after all, the end-game of a federal solution to the Indian Question—that Ottawa, to quote one official, "simply cannot afford to see it fail."

There are no assurances that Nisga'a self-government implementation will go smoothly, no guarantees that the communities involved will find it an easy task. There will be difficulties, to be sure. No social experiment of this scale can be expected to proceed without conflicts, controversies and administrative errors. Oppression damages people and it remains to be seen, as events are played out over the years, whether the Nisga'a can transform themselves into an

Many Nisga'a students take part in school music programs at Nisga'a Elementary Secondary School. Brass bands play energetically at many Nisga'a feasts and other functions. *Gary Fiegehen photo* autonomous, self-actualizing people under the treaty, or simply become the caretakers of their own dependency. Much time—at least three generations—may be needed to measure the success of a treaty that has the potential to change the course of Canadian history.

Contemplating the areas in which things could go wrong, Frank Calder says, "Rivalry between the four Nisga'a clans can at times lead to favouritism. It is common among so many tribal groups right across British Columbia. We're potlatch people; ours was a competitive system. But today, the Nisga'a people face a series of more competitions—from the outside world. This sets up a remarkable tension, because without the clan system we have no culture." But Thomas Berger points out that under the treaty the Nisga'a are no longer victims. "The time for rhetoric, speech making, and lawsuits is over," he says. "The Nisga'a now have to shift to a new set of realities. They will now have to get down to the donkey work necessary to build their own institutions and their own economy."

Berger is right. Successful implementation of the treaty implies cataclysmic change for the Nisga'a people. Over time, some may be disappointed when their new government enacts laws and makes policy decisions they do not like. In the past, civil servants from Ottawa and Victoria made convenient scapegoats. Today, in the small communities along the Nass, where powerful families could create oligarchies that would dominate government and employment, the Nisga'a Lisims Government, like governments around the world, may make poor choices and unwise investments. Who then to blame?

In one sense the treaty is a success *by its very existence*. An anomaly of time and place, it represents a political experiment on a grand scale and stands as a towering tribute to a people who refused to give up. It corrects a grievous historical error and provides a modest amount of land and money the Nisga'a people will need for economic development. The treaty also provides a municipal-plus model of self-government that allows the Nisga'a people to protect their traditional culture and manage their own affairs, and it establishes the Nisga'a polity in its own jurisdictions, in the same way that the city of Vancouver and the province of British Columbia are vested with their own distinct jurisdictions.

Over the years, politics in the Nass River Valley will likely remain a hybrid, an electorate in pursuit of a democratic meritocracy on the one hand, while on the other, a traditional system of hereditary chieftains and powerful family-based oligarchies. And if as expected more Nisga'a people return to live in the Nass—currently about 60 percent of the total Nisga'a population of 6,000 live outside the Nass in Terrace, Prince Rupert and Vancouver—they will bring with them new attitudes when it comes to issues such as women's rights. Even for a Nisga'a woman like Esther Adams, who has remained in the Nass Valley, the lack of women in Nisga'a politics is troubling, and she hints that one day she might run for office herself. With an insistent edge to her voice, she expresses the frustration of many young Nisga'a women who have been educated for something better than to serve male tribal bosses. "We must have more women in our political life. Today, we have a few, but not near enough." And it is hard to imagine a young Nisga'a woman raised in Vancouver, watching on television the political ascendancy of leaders such as Wendy Grant-John and Hillary Clinton, who would willingly revert to a subordinate role simply because she returns to the Nass River.

But if past behaviour predicts, there is good reason for a cautious optimism. Nisga'a leaders like Joseph Gosnell have shown themselves to be tenacious pragmatists, duty bound to protect and revitalize a traditional culture, while at the same time actively participating in the modern world beyond the lava beds of the Nass River. He and his wife are fiercely proud of their children. Son Keith Andrew, a graduate of the University of British Columbia, teaches elementary school in Terrace. Ted, a graduate of University of Northern British Columbia, works as a bookkeeper for the new Nisga'a government, and Joseph Jr. works in the aboriginal banking division of the Royal Bank, the primary financial institution for Nisga'a Lisims Government. Marilyn is an office worker and Sharon is a homemaker in Terrace. This past summer, the two youngest sons, Kevin and Frank, set out on their father's gillnetter to catch salmon near the mouth of the Skeena River. And in her spotless living room, Adele Gosnell has poured coffee for Prime Minister Chrétien and Premier Clark and dozens of other politicians and senior officials as well as the Canadian bureau chief for the *New York Times* and a German documentary film crew.

Despite a series of very public declarations that he would retire once the treaty was ratified, on September 18, 2000, Gosnell made a surprise decision to accept the nomination to run as president in the November 8, 2000, Nisga'a Lisims Government election, in which he was re-elected handily. Edmond Wright, who was elected secretary-treasurer of the new government, had approached Gosnell on several occasions after the treaty was ratified, urging him not to retire. "Now we have a treaty, we have to implement it," Wright said later. "We need a strong team. We need consistency because there is so much to be done."

The contrast between the Nisga'a way and that of other aboriginal peoples of Canada was never clearer than at the First Nations Summit in Prince Rupert, held in September, 2000. The keynote speaker, Chief Matthew Coon Come, the fiery leader of the Assembly of First Nations, spoke of the explosive fishing dispute in Burnt Church, New Brunswick, just the latest flashpoint in a series of ugly resource conflicts between aboriginal and non-aboriginal people. It wasn't the first and it won't be the last, Coon Come suggested to the assembled chiefs. But the rage and divisiveness that has followed in the wake of Burnt Church confirmed to Gosnell that the Nisga'a Treaty, with its negotiated settlement, offers a real-world solution to the crisis of aboriginal rights that is poisoning relations between neighbours and threatening the social order across Canada. Despite its many contradictions, the Nisga'a Treaty brings into sharp focus the question of

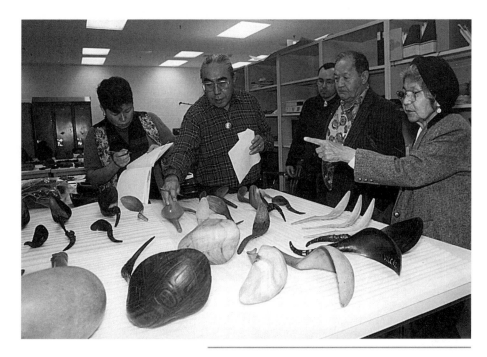

A group of elders helps Harry Nyce identify Nisga'a artifacts. Under the treaty about 300 artifacts are being repatriated to the Nisga'a.
Gary Fiegehen photo

how two cultures can live together and offers a peaceful solution to a long-standing grievance that could never have been settled by armed confronation.

Afterwards, relaxed and almost jaunty, Joseph Gosnell left the convention for a short drive to the nearby fishing village of Port Edward where, for the first time in seven years, he climbed aboard the *Nisga'a Cloud*, his eleven-metre gillnetter that was collecting barnacles at the end of the wharf. Poking about the deck, noting as all mariners do the myriad tasks that needed to be done, he took off his sports jacket and disappeared into the wheelhouse. A few minutes later, as the afternoon sun came slanting through the wheelhouse like a great slab of butter, he re-emerged with a smile on his face. Once again he was a young man and, with big brother James at the helm, the two Gosnell boys were setting out to sea, to ride—just one more time—the heaving motion of the *Nisga'a Cloud* as it hit the swells off Iceberg Bay.

Brooding and mysterious, the Nass River viewed upriver from Gitwinksihlkw. Since the last great Ice Age, the Nisga'a travelled, fished and settled along all 380 kilometres of the river and its tributaries.
Gary Fiegehen photo

Joe Gosnell answers treaty critics
Naysayers labour under misconceptions

Doubters of the Nisga'a deal are harbouring illusions about the powers and rights it grants.

Many opponents of the proposed Nisga'a treaty have based their arguments on misinformation, distortion and fear.

The BC government's advertising campaign did not respond in detail to opponents' many erroneous statements, while senior federal politicians have, until very recently, been almost completely silent. The press, with few exceptions, has concentrated on reporting the criticisms and conflict but not correcting the inaccuracies.

As the debate in the provincial legislature proceeds, it is necessary to attempt to correct at least some of the misrepresentations.

1. The Nisga'a treaty is not the result of a recent initiative, nor were negotiations a matter of mere policy.

   The Nisga'a people and other First Nations in BC have sought negotiated treaties ever since Europeans first arrived. The Nisga'a have persisted in our struggle ever since. Our trips to Victoria, our petition to the Privy Council in 1913 and our litigation resulting in the 1973 Supreme Court of Canada decision in *Calder v. Attorney General of British Columbia*, have all led to the negotiating table in 1976.

   Other developments have vindicated our quest including the constitutional recognition and affirmation of our existing aboriginal rights. The courts have made it abundantly clear that the negotiation of treaties is not something to be done at the whim of federal or provincial politicians. It is not a partisan political choice, it is a constitutional and moral obligation, rooted in the history and legal system of our country.

2. The Nisga'a treaty is not a "Glen Clark deal." It is a tripartite agreement that has been under negotiation between the Nisga'a Tribal Council and the

federal government since 1976. British Columbia joined negotiations in 1990 under Social Credit premier Bill Vander Zalm.

The Nisga'a treaty reflects many years of discussions with federal and provincial governments of all political stripes. The only constant has been the Nisga'a leadership.

3. The Nisga'a final agreement is not primarily an agreement between the Nisga'a and British Columbia.

Canada, not British Columbia, has primary responsibility for treaty making. The *Constitution Act*, 1867 assigns exclusive jurisdiction over "Indians, and lands reserved for Indians" to the federal government. Historically, provincial governments were not parties to treaties and many First Nations still totally reject any provincial involvement in the negotiations.

Because the province owns public lands and title to many resources and because aboriginal title constitutes an interest to which provincial Crown title is subject, it was considered necessary and desirable to include the province as a full party to the Nisga'a treaty.

However, the federal government's primary role is reflected by the fact that most of the money and the principal authority regarding Nisga'a government, fiscal arrangements and fisheries, comes from Canada.

4. The Nisga'a final agreement is not a "template."

Opponents, who refer to the "Nisga'a template" and not the "Nisga'a treaty," insist the Nisga'a agreement will be applied like a cookie cutter in all of the other negotiations under way in the province. This suggestion would be too absurd to be taken seriously if it were not being repeated so frequently.

The Nisga'a Tribal Council had neither the desire nor the mandate to negotiate for anyone other than the Nisga'a nation.

5. The Nisga'a treaty will not establish an "enclave."

In her column in *The Vancouver Sun* on Nov. 17, Barbara Yaffe repeated the claim the Nisga'a treaty raises issues "like ghettoizing native people by creating enclaves." Oxford defines an "enclave" as "foreign territory surrounded by one's own territory." Nisga'a land (the main parcel of land to be owned as an estate in fee simple by the Nisga'a nation) can in no way be described as "foreign territory." The treaty makes it clear all federal and provincial laws, including the Charter of Rights and Freedoms, apply to Nisga'a lands.

One of our fundamental goals is to negotiate our way into Canada. It is mischievous to say that the result is the creation of foreign territory within Canada or to characterize the limited area of our territory as a "ghetto."

6. Nisga'a government will not have jurisdiction over land currently owned by non-Nisga'a within the Nass Valley.

Recent articles in *The Vancouver Sun* and elsewhere have suggested that non-Nisga'a residents will be subject to Nisga'a government jurisdiction, while being denied the ability to run or vote for Nisga'a government. This is simply wrong. All of the existing fee simple properties are expressly excluded from Nisga'a lands. Residents will continue to have the right to vote for federal, provincial and regional governments.

These residents already have a level of representation on the Nisga'a Valley health board and on the district school board far in excess of their numbers. This participation would continue and if those bodies were replaced by institutions created by Nisga'a government, some means of ensuring their participation would be provided. There is no authority for the Nisga'a government to tax these people or their properties.

7. Virtually all Nisga'a government laws will be restricted to Nisga'a citizens and Nisga'a lands.

The laws that can be made, with a very few well-defined exceptions, deal with Nisga'a citizens, Nisga'a treaty rights and Nisga'a property.

The treaty would limit Nisga'a government authority to "laws to preserve, promote, and develop Nisga'a culture and Nisga'a language." It expressly does not include the authority to make laws in respect of intellectual property, the official languages of Canada or prohibition of activities outside Nisga'a lands.

Why do people such as Bill Vander Zalm, Gordon Campbell and Melvin Smith believe that federal or provincial laws should prevail over Nisga'a laws in respect of Nisga'a language or Nisga'a culture?

Do they really wish to retain the ability to undermine First Nations' languages and cultures in the future, as their predecessors did in the past?

Nisga'a government can make laws that prevail over federal and provincial laws regarding its own administration, management and operation. However, any Nisga'a law inconsistent with the treaty is invalid. The treaty requires the Nisga'a government to meet fundamental standards of democratic and financial accountability and comply with the charter.

There are many areas over which the Nisga'a government will have no authority including criminal law, industrial relations and accreditation or certification of professions and trades.

8. The treaty does not deny anyone democratic rights.

Almost all Nisga'a government jurisdiction is restricted to Nisga'a citizens and Nisga'a lands.

However, Nisga'a citizenship and the ability to participate in Nisga'a government is not restricted to persons who meet the eligibility criteria. Nisga'a government has the authority to grant citizenship to people, extending to them the rights and responsibilities of all Nisga'a citizens.

The Nisga'a insisted on this power in recognition that there will be residents who are, in every meaningful way, full members of the communities and should be included in the democratic functions of Nisga'a government.

If the activities of Nisga'a government or its institutions significantly and directly affect non-Nisga'a residents, the treaty requires involvement—from consultation to the right to vote or be guaranteed representation—depending on the nature of the activity and its effect on other people.

The issue of non-Nisga'a participation is not a simple one that can be solved by facile slogans about equality or by forcing Nisga'a people to have internal decisions about our rights determined by the wishes of non-Nisga'a.

9. Nisga'a government is not an "order of government" equivalent to the federal or provincial governments, nor is it equivalent to a municipal government.

The treaty recognizes the right to self-government and provides authority to make laws. This right is recognized and affirmed by Section 35 of the *Constitution Act*, 1982. However, this constitutional protection is not the same as the constitutional entrenchment of the federal and provincial governments.

The Nisga'a government would not have any exclusive jurisdiction. All existing federal and provincial jurisdiction will continue to apply. However, Nisga'a laws will also apply—something that is known as "concurrent jurisdiction." This is very common in Canada, as federal, provincial and municipal laws often overlap, despite the establishment of exclusive jurisdictions.

Whoever thinks the Nisga'a or any other First Nation will return to the negotiating table to accept whatever crumbs people like Gordon Campbell or Bill Vander Zalm are willing to offer must face the reality that this will not happen.

The proposed treaty is a balanced and sensible reconciliation of issues that have frustrated and divided British Columbians for more than a century. It should be celebrated as the proof that people of good faith can resolve their differences without confrontation or litigation.

Joseph Gosnell
President, Nisga'a Tribal Council

1579	Sir Francis Drake claims the West Coast for England.
1742	Russians start trading on Northwest Coast.
c.1774	2,000 Nisga'a killed when trapped in a lava flow after a volcano erupts in Nass Valley.
1831	Hudson's Bay Company established at Fort (Port) Simpson on Nass River. Abandoned three years later.
1858	Colony of British Columbia established. First Christian sermon preached to the Nass Indians in their language.
1864	Mission founded at Gingolx (Kincolith); 1878 mission founded at Gitlakdamiks (New Aiyansh).
1860, 1869	Nisga'a fight neighbouring tribe to win control of river fishery.
1870	BC unilaterally denies existence of aboriginal title, claiming aboriginal people are too primitive to understand concept of land ownership.
1876	Ottawa agrees not to discuss aboriginal title before establishing reserves for Indians.
1878	Canada begins to restrict traditional Indian fishing rights, making a new distinction between food and commercial fishing.
1881	First cannery built on Nass River.
1884	*Indian Act* amended to outlaw cultural and religious ceremonies such as the potlatch.
1885	Three Nisga'a chiefs travel to Ottawa and meet with Prime Minister John A. Macdonald.
1886	Nisga'a chief Sgat'iin refuses entry to provincial government surveyors.
1887	Nisga'a and Tsimshian chiefs travel to Victoria to demand the negotiation of treaties concerning changes in their sovereignty over traditional lands.
1889	Federal system of permits introduced to govern commercial fishing. Indians are effectively excluded from commercial fishing.

1890	Nisga'a establish their first Land Committee.
1909	Nisga'a Land Committee joins with other North Coast tribes to form the Native Tribes of BC.
1910	Prime Minister Wilfrid Laurier, visiting Prince Rupert, promises to resolve the Indian land question. The initiative dies with his electoral defeat in 1911.
1913	Nisga'a petition the British Privy Council for treaties and self-government in accordance with the principles set out in the Royal Proclamation of 1763. Petition referred back to Canada.
1920	Compulsory attendance of Indian children in schools.
1923	Ottawa grants Indians the right to take up commercial fishing.
1924	The McKenna-McBride Commission allots the Nisga'a 76 square kilometres of reserve land from their traditional territories of almost 25,000 square kilometres.
1927	Ottawa prohibits Indians from organizing to discuss land claims.
1931	Native Brotherhood of BC is formed. Secret discussions are launched to keep the Indian land question alive.
1949	Nisga'a chief Frank Calder is elected to the BC Legislature.
1951	Parliament repeals provisions of the *Indian Act* that outlawed the potlatch and prohibited land claims activity.
1955	The Nisga'a Land Committee is re-established as the Nisga'a Tribal Council.
1960	Aboriginal people on reserves granted the right to vote in federal elections. Phasing out of Indian residential schools begins.
1968	Nisga'a take the land question to court.
1973	Calder Decision: The Supreme Court of Canada rules that the Nisga'a had held aboriginal title before settlers came, but the judges split evenly on the question of the continuing existence of their title. Jean Chrétien, minister of Indian

	Affairs, announces federal intention to settle claims.
1976	Nisga'a begin negotiations with Ottawa to settle land claims.
1982	Constitution of Canada recognizes and affirms aboriginal title.
1990	BC government joins Nisga'a treaty negotiations.
1991	BC government recognizes both aboriginal title and the inherent Nisga'a right to self-government, and a tripartite framework agreement is signed.
1992	BC/Canada/First Nations Summit establishes the BC Treaty Commission.
1996, Feb. 22	Agreement in principle (AIP) is initialled by negotiators from Canada, BC and the Nisga'a Tribal Council and signed March 22, 1996.
1998, Aug. 4	Final Agreement initialled in Gitlakdamiks.
1998, Nov. 7	Final Agreement ratified by Nisga'a people.
1998, Nov. 30	Nisga'a Final Agreement Act (Bill 51) introduced in BC Legislature.
1998, Dec. 2	Chief Gosnell addresses BC Legislature to begin debate on Bill 51.
1999, Apr. 22	Using closure, Bill 51 passes British Columbia Legislature.
1999, Apr. 26	Bill 51 is given Royal Assent in Victoria.
1999, May 4	Final Agreement signed in Ottawa.
1999, Oct. 19	Bill C-9 (Nisga'a) introduced in House of Commons.
1999, Dec. 13	Bill passes in House of Commons by a vote of 217–48.
1999, Dec. 14	Bill referred to Canadian Senate.
2000, April 13	Senate approves the bill on third reading. Nisga'a Treaty is formally ratified and given Royal Assent.
2000, May 11	Nisga'a Lisims Government comes into effect; passes its first eighteen laws.
2000, May 12	Nisga'a celebrate treaty ratification in Gitwinksihlkw.
2000, Sept. 14	New legislative building, Wilpsi'ayuukhl Nisga'a, opens as formal seat of Nisga'a self-government.

APPENDIX 3:
THE COST OF THE NISGA'A TREATY
(all figures in 1999 dollars)

The Nisga'a will receive the cash sum of $196.1 million over a fifteen-year period

Funding to increase Nisga'a participation in the commercial fishing industry through the purchase of vessels and licences: $11.8 million

Transition, training and other one-time implementation funding paid over five years: $40.6 million

Forestry transition funding: estimated $4.5 million

Canada's contribution to the Lisims Fisheries Conservation Trust to support fisheries science on the Nass River: $10.3 million

Canada's contribution to BC to assist those who may be affected by the treaty: $3.2 million

Surveys: $3.1 million

Purchase of third party interests: $30.0 million

Cost to British Columbia to pave the Nisga'a Highway: $41.4 million

The province of British Columbia has ascribed values to Nisga'a Lands and fee simple parcels, totalling 2,019 square kilometres: $108.6 million

Foregone forest revenues: $37.5 million

Total estimated cost of the Nisga'a Treaty: $487.1 million

Of this amount, the Canadian government will pay $255 million, the British Columbia government $232.1 million

Bibliography

Ames, Kenneth M. and Herbert D.G. Maschner. *Peoples of the Northwest Coast: Their Archaeology and Prehistory*. London: Thames & Hudson, 1999.

Bachelard, Michael. *The Great Land Grab*. Victoria, Australia: Hyland House Publishing, 1997.

Barman, Jean. *The West Beyond the West: A History of British Columbia*. Toronto: University of Toronto Press, 1996.

Berger, Thomas. *A Long and Terrible Shadow: White Values and Native Rights in the Americas Since 1492*. Vancouver: Douglas & McIntyre, 1999.

Berlo, Janet C. and Ruth B. Phillips. *Native North American Art*. Oxford, New York: Oxford University Press, 1998.

Bryan, Liz. *British Columbia: This Favoured Land*. Vancouver: Douglas & McIntyre, 1982.

Cole, Douglas. *Captured Heritage: The Scramble for Northwest Coast Artifacts*. Vancouver: University of BC Press, 1995.

Duff, Wilson. *The Indian History of British Columbia: The Impact of the White Man*. Victoria: Royal British Columbia Museum, 1997.

Fisher, Robin. *Contact and Conflict: Indian-European Relations in British Columbia, 1774-1890*. Vancouver: University of BC Press, 1997.

Flanagan, Tom. *First Nations? Second Thoughts*. Montreal: McGill-Queen's University Press, 2000.

Francis, Daniel. *The Imaginary Indian: The Image of the Indian in Canadian Culture*. Vancouver: Arsenal Pulp Press, 1992.

Glavin, Terry. *The Last Great Sea: A Voyage Through the Human and Natural History of the North Pacific Ocean*. Vancouver: Greystone Books, 2000.

Glavin, Terry. *This Ragged Place: Travels Across the Landscape*. Vancouver: New Star Books, 1996.

Heizer, R.F., Robert H. Lowie, Edward W. Gifford, Philip
    Drucker and R.L. Olson. "Northwest Coast." *Cultural Element
    Distributions*, No. XXVI, Coyote Press, 1950.

Holm, Bill. *Northwest Coast Art: An Analysis of Form.* Seattle:
    University of Washington Press, 1965.

Kunin, Roslyn, ed. *Prospering Together: The Economic Impact of the
    Aboriginal Title Settlements in BC.* Vancouver: The Laurier
    Institution, 1998.

Raunet, Daniel. *Without Surrender, Without Consent: A History of
    the Nishga Land Claims.* Vancouver: Douglas & McIntyre,
    1984.

Rayner, William. *British Columbia Premiers in Profile: The Good, the
    Bad and the Transient.* Surrey, BC: Heritage House, 2000.

Rose, Alex. *Bringing Our Ancestors Home: The Repatriation of
    Nisga'a Artifacts.* New Aiyansh, BC: Nisga'a Tribal Council,
    1998.

Rose, Alex. *Nisga'a: People of the Nass River.* Vancouver: Douglas
    & McIntyre, 1993.

Simpson, Jeffrey. *Faultlines: Struggling for a Canadian Vision.*
    Toronto: HarperCollins, 1993.

Smith, Mel. *Our Home or Native Land: What Government's
    Aboriginal Policy Is Doing to Canada.* Toronto: Stoddart
    Publishing, 1996.

Tennant, Paul. *Aboriginal Peoples and Politics: The Indian Land
    Question in British Columbia.* Vancouver: University of BC
    Press, 1990.

Woodcock, George. *British Columbia: A History of the Province.*
    Vancouver: Douglas & McIntyre, 1990.